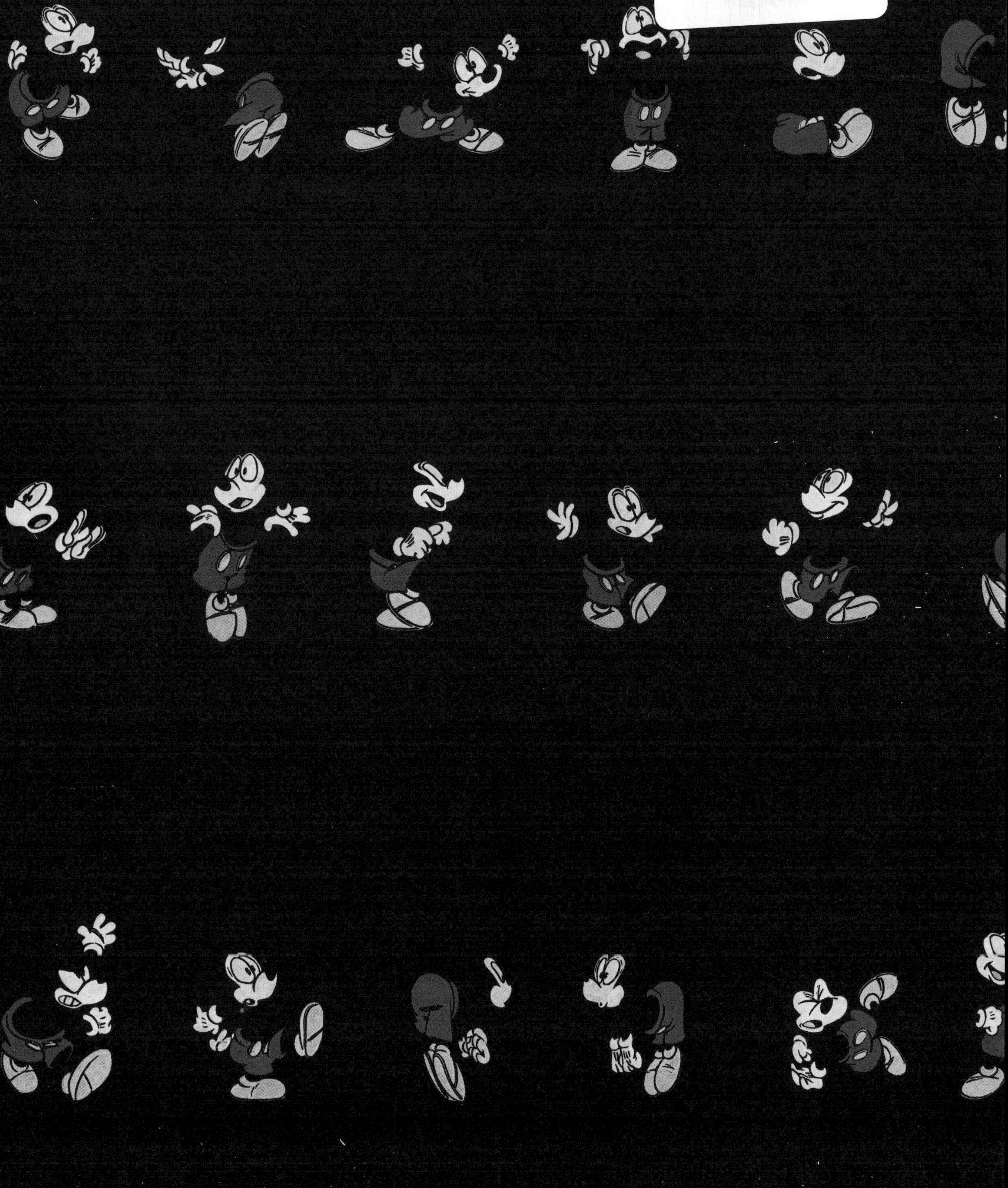

Walt Disney

Mickey and Donald

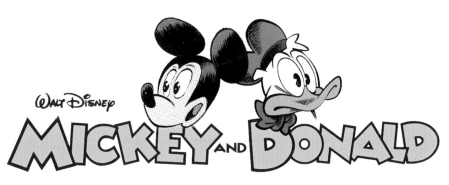

Mickey's Craziest Adventures

STORY

LEWIS TRONDHEIM

ART

NICOLAS KERAMIDAS

COLOR

BRIGITTE FINDAKLY

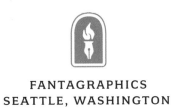

FANTAGRAPHICS

SEATTLE, WASHINGTON

Publisher: GARY GROTH
Editor: DAVID GERSTEIN
Translator: IVANKA HAHNENBERGER
Dialogue: DAVID GERSTEIN
Designer: JUSTIN ALLAN-SPENCER and ÉDITIONS GLÉNAT
Lettering: DERON BENNETT with PAUL BARESH
Production: C HWANG
Associate Publisher/VP: ERIC REYNOLDS

Fantagraphics Books, Inc.
7563 Lake City Way NE
Seattle WA 98115
(800) 657-1100

Visit us at fantagraphics.com
Follow us on Twitter at @fantagraphics
and on Facebook at facebook.com/fantagraphics.

First printing: January 2024
ISBN 978-1-68396-926-6
Printed in China

The feature story in this volume was first published in France in 2016.
This edition is adapted from the first American edition, released in 2017.

IN THIS SERIES

Mickey Mouse: Mickey All-Stars | 40 international artists, including Giorgio Cavazzano and Mike Peraza

Mickey Mouse: Zombie Coffee | Régis Loisel

Donald Duck: Donald's Happiest Adventures | Lewis Trondheim and Nicolas Keramidas

Scrooge McDuck: The Dragon of Glasgow | Joris Chamblain and Fabrizio Petrossi

Mickey and Donald: Mickey's Craziest Adventures | Lewis Trondheim and Nicolas Keramidas

THE COMPLETE CARL BARKS DISNEY LIBRARY

Walt Disney's Donald Duck: Maharajah Donald | Vol. 4

Walt Disney's Uncle Scrooge: Cave of Ali Baba | Vol. 23

DISNEY AFTERNOON ADVENTURES

TaleSpin: Flight of the Sky-Raker | Bobbi JG Weiss, Michael T. Gilbert, Romano Scarpa, and others; Vol. 2

Chip 'n Dale Rescue Rangers: The Count Roquefort Case | Bobbi JG Weiss, Doug Gray, Lee Nordling, and others; Vol. 3

Adventures of the Gummi Bears: A New Beginning | Doug Gray, Philippe Gasc, Maximino Tortajada Aguilar, and others; Vol. 4

DISNEY MASTERS

Mickey Mouse: The Monster of Sawtooth Mountain | Paul Murry; Vol. 21

Uncle Scrooge: Operation Galleon Grab | Giorgio Cavazzano; Vol. 22

Mickey Mouse: The Riddle of Brigaboom | Romano Scarpa; Vol. 23

Uncle Scrooge: World Wide Witch | Daniel Branca; Vol. 24

SILLY SYMPHONIES

Walt Disney's Silly Symphonies 1932-1935 Starring Bucky Bug and Donald Duck
Al Taliaferro with Earl Duvall, Merrill De Maris, and Ted Osborne

Walt Disney's Silly Symphonies 1935-1939 Starring Donald Duck and the Big Bad Wolf | Al Taliaferro with Carl Barks, Merrill De Maris, and Ted Osborne

ALSO AVAILABLE

Disney Comics: Around the World in One Hundred Years | 20+ international creators, including Carl Barks, Floyd Gottfredson, Daan Jippes, Freddy Milton, Don Rosa, and Romano Scarpa | Target Stores exclusive

Disney One Saturday Morning Adventures | 40+ international creators, including Daan Jippes, Laura McCreary, and Scott Gimple

Mickey and Donald: For Whom the Doorbell Tolls and Other Tales Inspired by Hemingway | 12 international creators, including Giorgio Cavazzano, Andrea Freccero, and Alessandro Perina; annotations and afterword by Robert K. Elder

Mickey and Donald Fantastic Futures | 15 international creators, including Mirka Andolfo, Francesco Artibani, Lorenzo Pastrovicchio, and Claudio Sciarrone

Uncle Scrooge and Donald Duck: Bear Mountain Tales
20 American and international artists, including Carl Barks, Don Rosa, Daniel Branca, and Giorgio Cavazzano

Uncle Scrooge and Donald Duck in Les Misérables and War and Peace
Giovan Battista Carpi

Walt Disney's Uncle Scrooge: The Diamond Jubilee Collection | Carl Barks with William Van Horn and Daan Jippes

FROM OUR NON-DISNEY CATALOG

Nuft and the Last Dragons: By Balloon to the North Pole | Freddy Milton

A FORGOTTEN TREASURE?

BY ÉDITIONS GLÉNAT
INTRODUCTION TO THE 2016 FRENCH EDITION

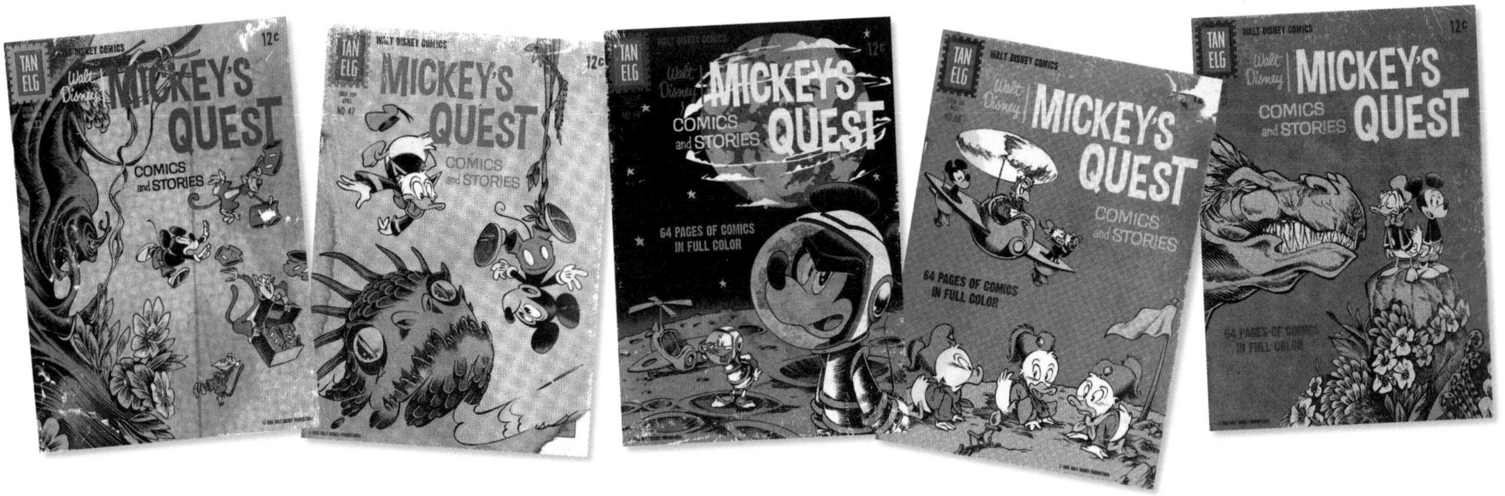
TAN ELG
12¢
MICKEY'S QUEST
COMICS and STORIES
TAN ELG
WALT DISNEY COMICS
MICKEY'S QUEST
COMICS and STORIES
12¢
TAN ELG
MICKEY'S QUEST
COMICS and STORIES
64 PAGES OF COMICS IN FULL COLOR
TAN ELG
WALT DISNEY COMICS
MICKEY'S QUEST
COMICS and STORIES
64 PAGES OF COMICS IN FULL COLOR
TAN ELG
WALT DISNEY COMICS
12¢
MICKEY'S QUEST
COMICS and STORIES

One beautiful spring Sunday, **Lewis Trondheim** and **Nicolas Keramidas** were meandering from table to table at a garage sale without looking for anything in particular — except, perhaps, for Keramidas, who never misses a chance to add to his vintage toy collection.

Then suddenly, as the two browsed halfheartedly through an old carton shoved into a corner, came the find of a century: about 40 issues of a comic from the 1960s that had been completely forgotten until now!

It was a collection — alas, not quite complete — of the comic book *Walt Disney's Comics and Stories: Mickey's Quest*, a rare spinoff title not archived at Disney and only ever distributed regionally. It included a gem never reissued, the famous "Mickey's Craziest Adventures" serial: a series of one-page installments that were published monthly and captivated young readers from May 1962 to February 1969.

Not able to keep this discovery to themselves, Lewis Trondheim and Nicolas Keramidas decided to share the serial chapters with today's readers. Lewis worked hard to adapt the humor of these masterpieces as best he could; Nicolas put all his talent to work at designing a cover worthy of the serial's superb artwork.

Alas, it is not possible to publish all of the pages of the serial, as some of them are feared lost forever. But the 44 pages recovered in this facsimile will allow the reader to enjoy the story's wonderful qualities.

(To those wayward souls who claim that the comic book *Walt Disney's Comics and Stories: Mickey's Quest* is really a figment of our imagination — a ploy to present a modern, newly-created serial in the guise of a rare 1960s fragment — we reply that the comics medium is an excellent place to keep your sense of humor.)

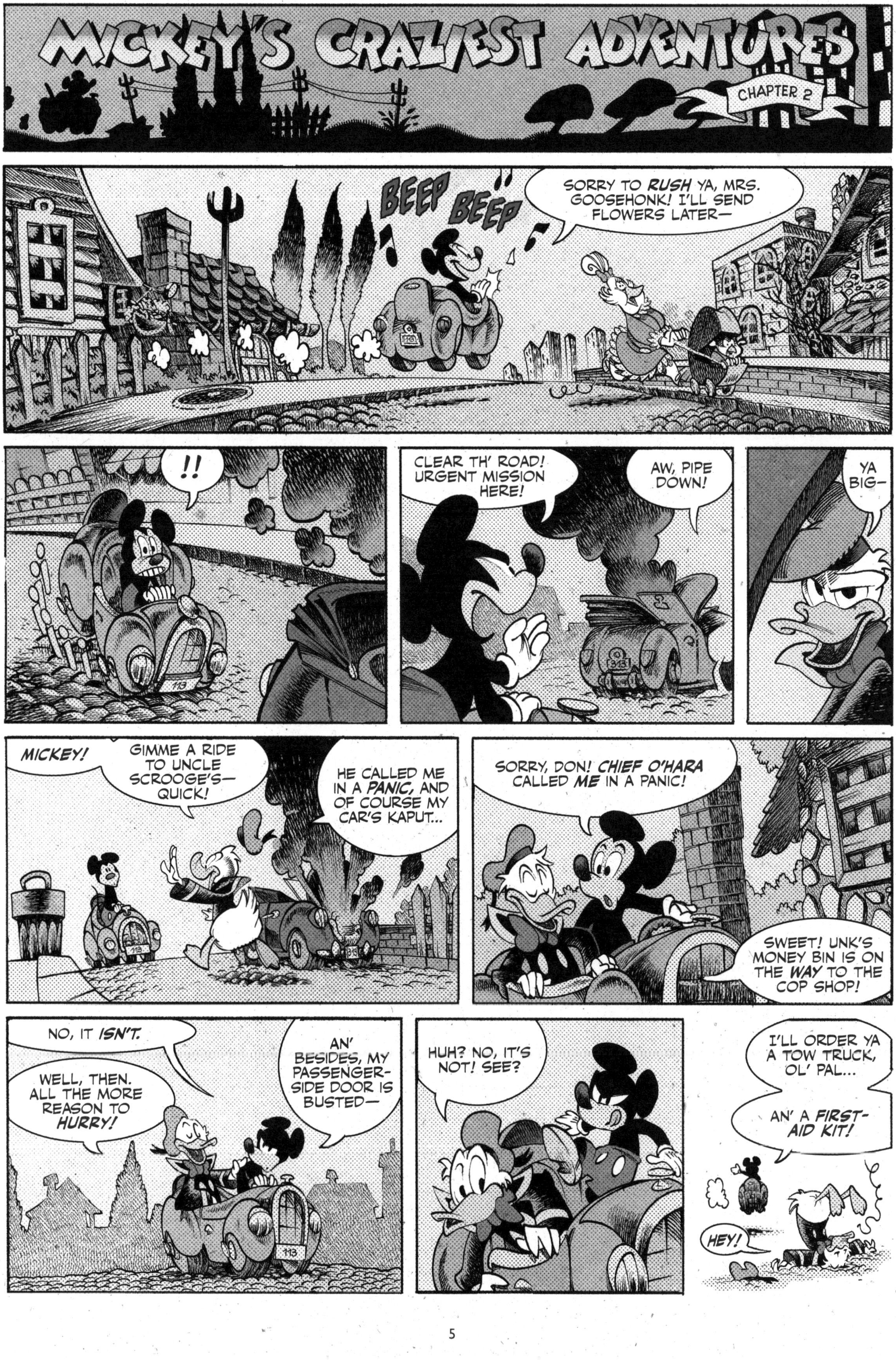
MICKEY'S CRAZIEST ADVENTURES
CHAPTER 2
BEEP BEEP
SORRY TO RUSH YA, MRS. GOOSEHONK! I'LL SEND FLOWERS LATER—
!!
CLEAR TH' ROAD! URGENT MISSION HERE!
AW, PIPE DOWN!
YA BIG—
MICKEY!
GIMME A RIDE TO UNCLE SCROOGE'S— QUICK!
HE CALLED ME IN A PANIC, AND OF COURSE MY CAR'S KAPUT...
SORRY, DON! CHIEF O'HARA CALLED ME IN A PANIC!
SWEET! UNK'S MONEY BIN IS ON THE WAY TO THE COP SHOP!
NO, IT ISN'T.
WELL, THEN. ALL THE MORE REASON TO HURRY!
AN' BESIDES, MY PASSENGER-SIDE DOOR IS BUSTED—
HUH? NO, IT'S NOT! SEE?
I'LL ORDER YA A TOW TRUCK, OL' PAL...
AN' A FIRST-AID KIT!
HEY!

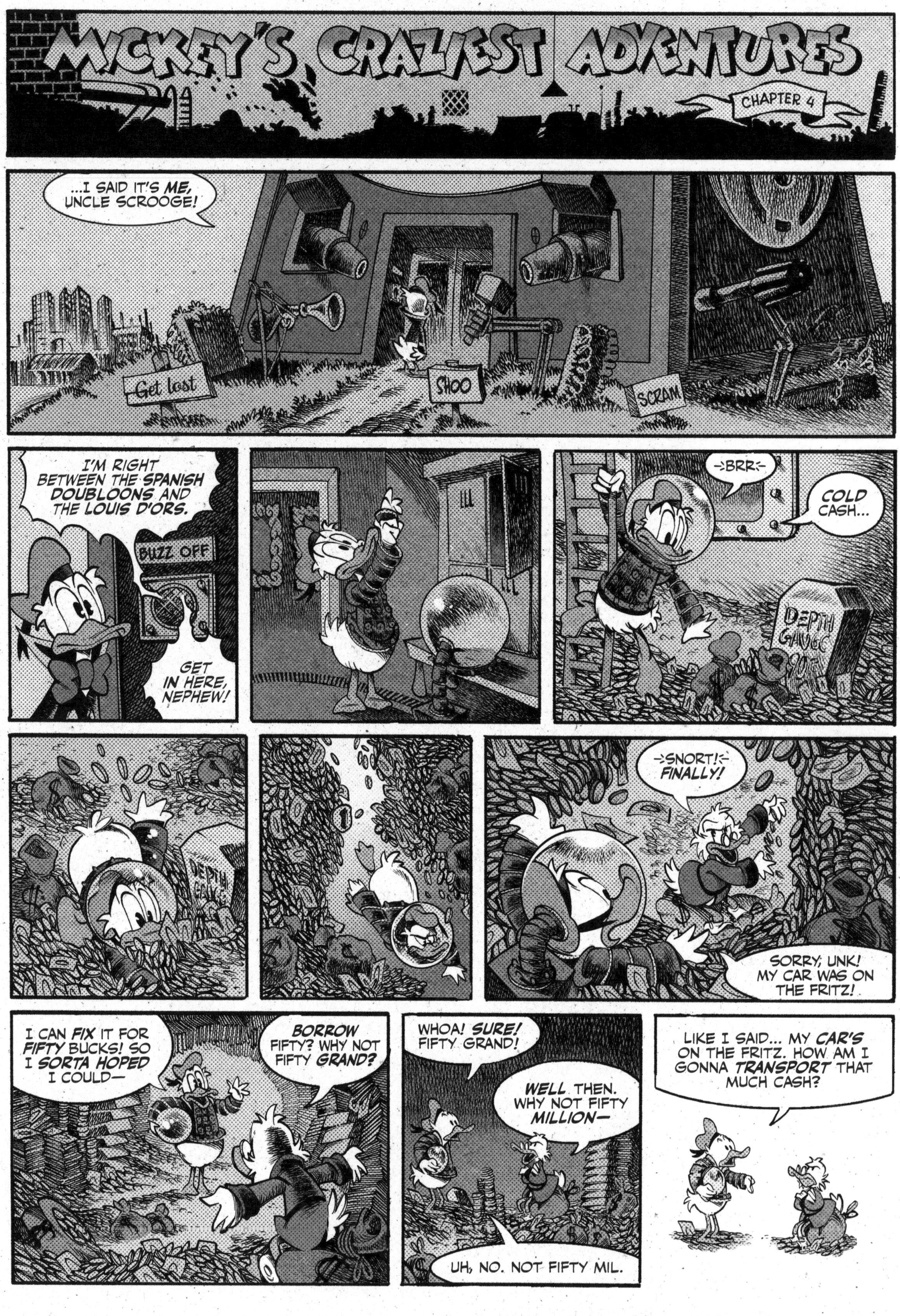
MICKEY'S CRAZIEST ADVENTURES
CHAPTER 4
...I SAID IT'S ME, UNCLE SCROOGE!
Get lost
SHOO
SCRAM
I'M RIGHT BETWEEN THE SPANISH DOUBLOONS AND THE LOUIS D'ORS.
BUZZ OFF
GET IN HERE, NEPHEW!
-BRR-
COLD CASH...
DEPTH GAUGE
-SNORT!- FINALLY!
SORRY, UNK! MY CAR WAS ON THE FRITZ!
I CAN FIX IT FOR FIFTY BUCKS! SO I SORTA HOPED I COULD—
BORROW FIFTY? WHY NOT FIFTY GRAND?
WHOA! SURE! FIFTY GRAND!
WELL THEN. WHY NOT FIFTY MILLION—
UH, NO. NOT FIFTY MIL.
LIKE I SAID... MY CAR'S ON THE FRITZ. HOW AM I GONNA TRANSPORT THAT MUCH CASH?

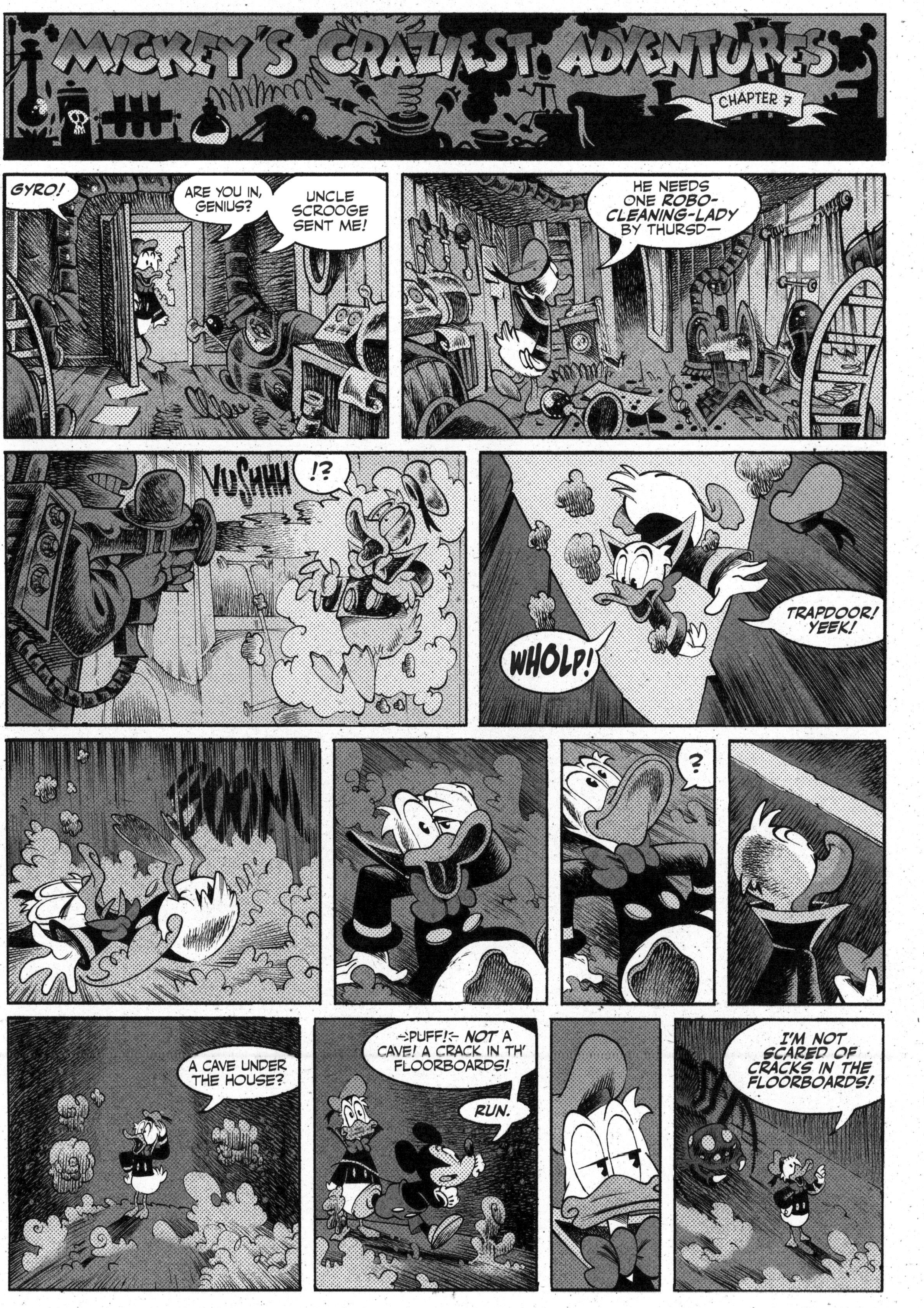
MICKEY'S CRAZIEST ADVENTURES
CHAPTER 7
GYRO!
ARE YOU IN, GENIUS?
UNCLE SCROOGE SENT ME!
HE NEEDS ONE *ROBO-CLEANING-LADY* BY THURSD—
VUSHHH
!?
WHOLP!
TRAPDOOR! YEEK!
?
A CAVE UNDER THE HOUSE?
—PUFF!— *NOT* A CAVE! A CRACK IN TH' FLOORBOARDS!
RUN.
I'M NOT SCARED OF CRACKS IN THE FLOORBOARDS!

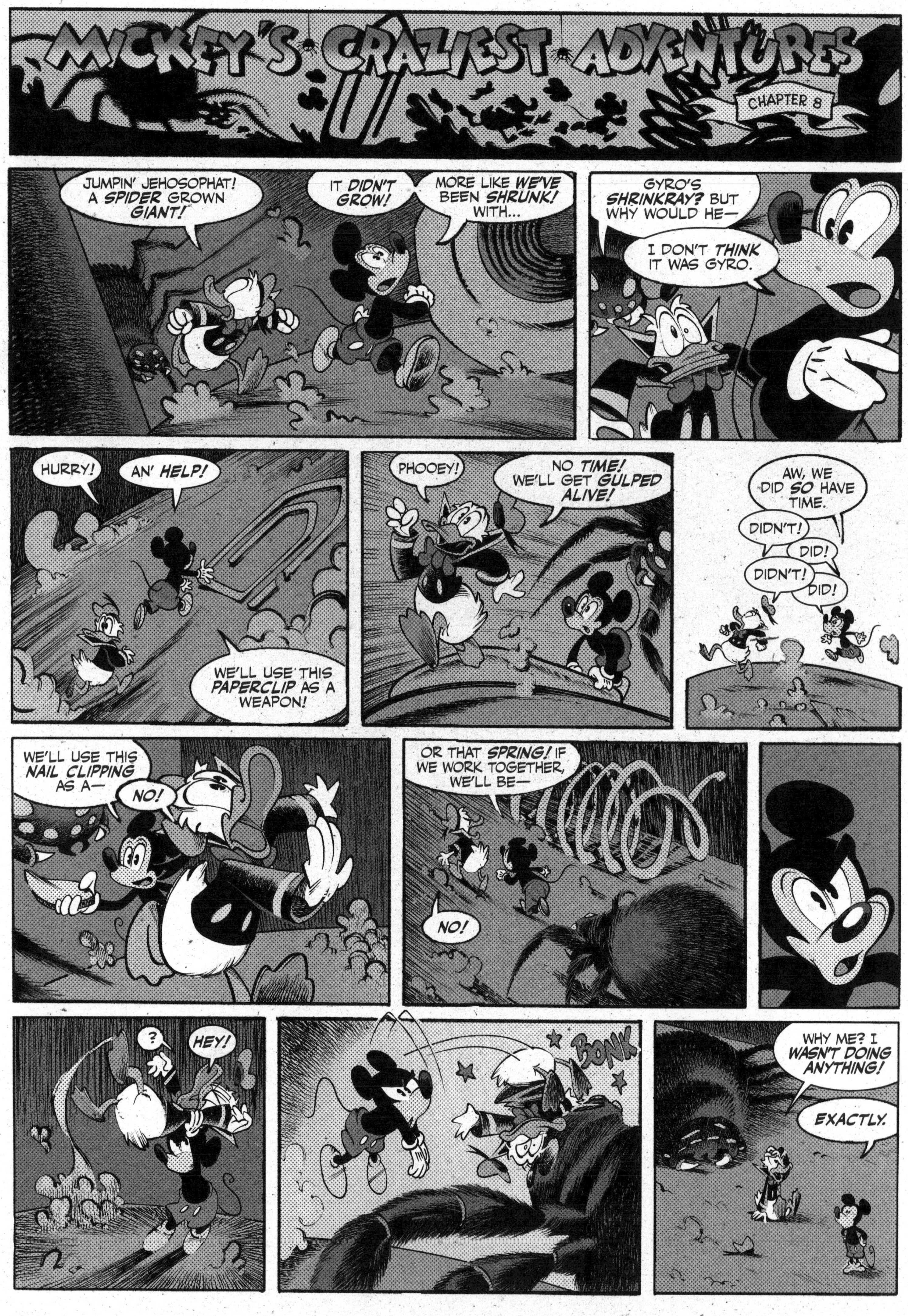

MICKEY'S CRAZIEST ADVENTURES
CHAPTER 8
JUMPIN' JEHOSOPHAT! A SPIDER GROWN GIANT!
IT DIDN'T GROW!
MORE LIKE WE'VE BEEN SHRUNK! WITH...
GYRO'S SHRINKRAY? BUT WHY WOULD HE—
I DON'T THINK IT WAS GYRO.
HURRY!
AN' HELP!
WE'LL USE THIS PAPERCLIP AS A WEAPON!
PHOOEY!
NO TIME! WE'LL GET GULPED ALIVE!
AW, WE DID SO HAVE TIME.
DIDN'T!
DID!
DIDN'T!
DID!
WE'LL USE THIS NAIL CLIPPING AS A—
NO!
OR THAT SPRING! IF WE WORK TOGETHER, WE'LL BE—
NO!
?
HEY!
BONK
WHY ME? I WASN'T DOING ANYTHING!
EXACTLY.

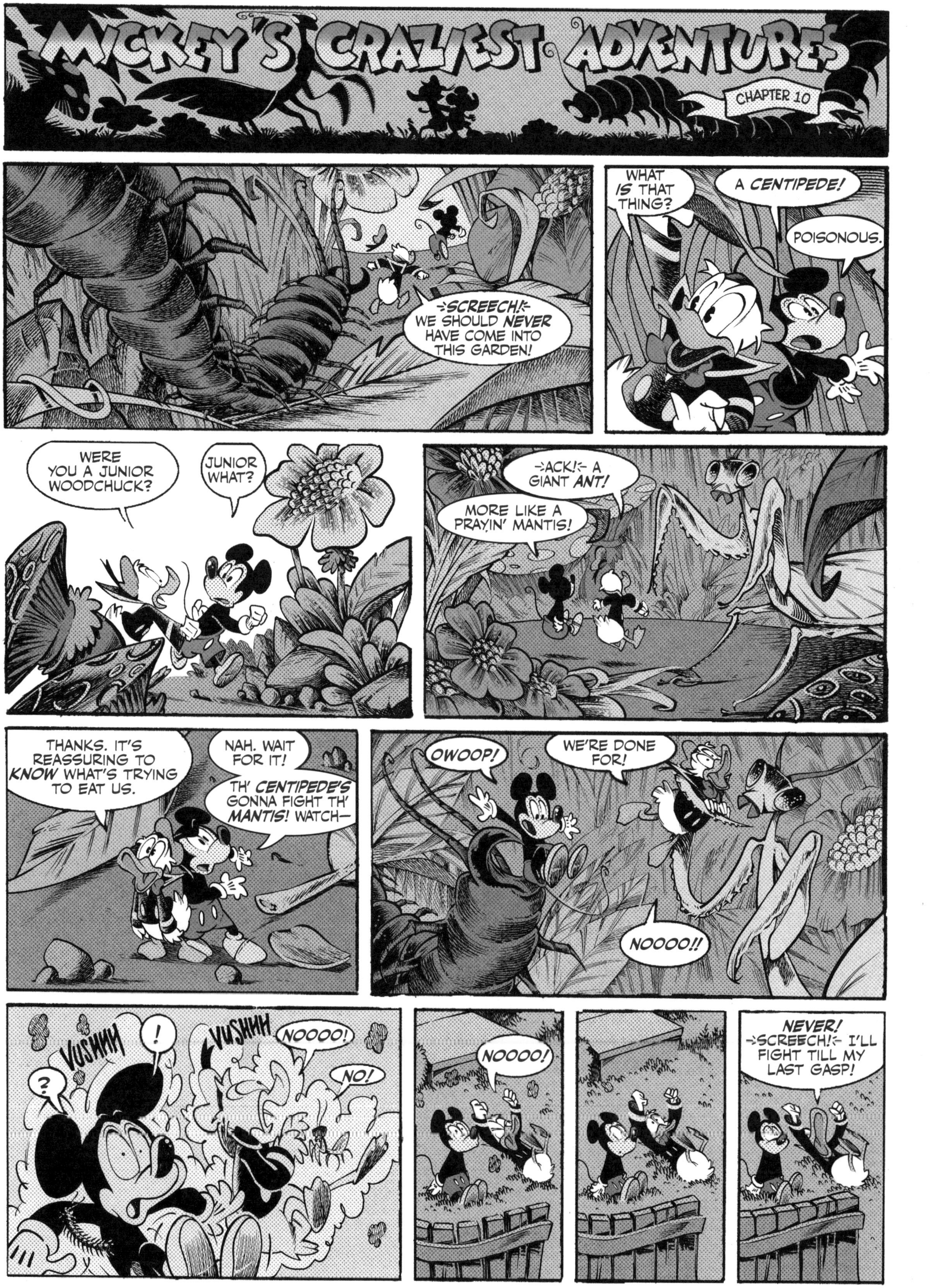
MICKEY'S CRAZIEST ADVENTURES
CHAPTER 10
-SCREECH!- WE SHOULD NEVER HAVE COME INTO THIS GARDEN!
WHAT IS THAT THING?
A CENTIPEDE!
POISONOUS.
WERE YOU A JUNIOR WOODCHUCK?
JUNIOR WHAT?
-ACK!- A GIANT ANT!
MORE LIKE A PRAY,IN' MANTIS!
THANKS. IT'S REASSURING TO KNOW WHAT'S TRYING TO EAT US.
NAH. WAIT FOR IT!
TH' CENTIPEDE'S GONNA FIGHT TH' MANTIS! WATCH—
OWOOP!
WE'RE DONE FOR!
NOOOO!!
VUSHHH
?
!
VUSHHH
NOOOO!
NO!
NOOOO!
NEVER! -SCREECH!- I'LL FIGHT TILL MY LAST GASP!

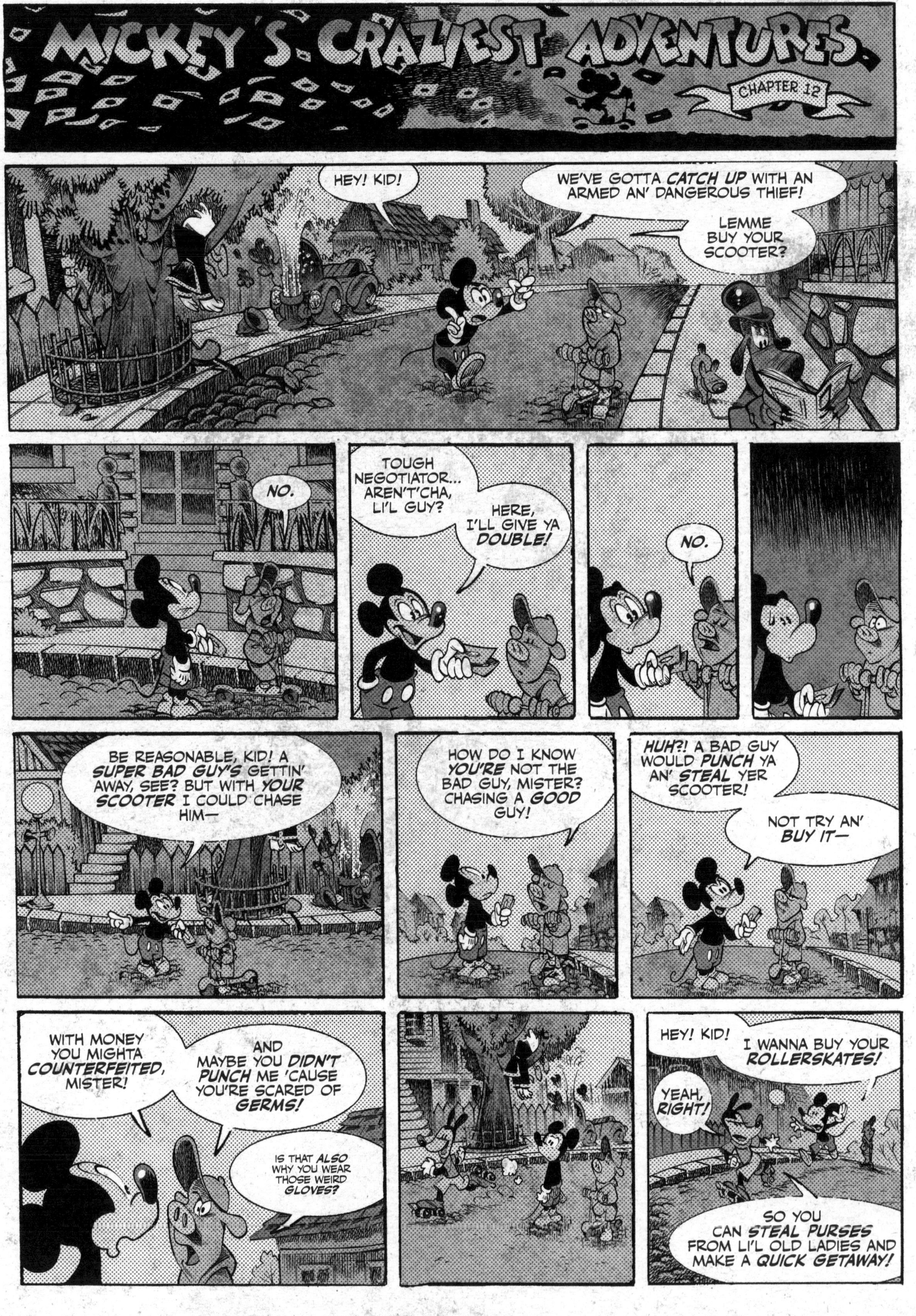
MICKEY'S CRAZIEST ADVENTURES
CHAPTER 12
HEY! KID!
WE'VE GOTTA CATCH UP WITH AN ARMED AN' DANGEROUS THIEF!
LEMME BUY YOUR SCOOTER?
NO.
TOUGH NEGOTIATOR... AREN'T'CHA, LI'L GUY?
HERE, I'LL GIVE YA DOUBLE!
NO.
BE REASONABLE, KID! A SUPER BAD GUY'S GETTIN' AWAY, SEE? BUT WITH YOUR SCOOTER I COULD CHASE HIM—
HOW DO I KNOW YOU'RE NOT THE BAD GUY, MISTER? CHASING A GOOD GUY!
HUH?! A BAD GUY WOULD PUNCH YA AN' STEAL YER SCOOTER!
NOT TRY AN' BUY IT—
WITH MONEY YOU MIGHTA COUNTERFEITED, MISTER!
AND MAYBE YOU DIDN'T PUNCH ME 'CAUSE YOU'RE SCARED OF GERMS!
IS THAT ALSO WHY YOU WEAR THOSE WEIRD GLOVES?
HEY! KID!
I WANNA BUY YOUR ROLLERSKATES!
YEAH, RIGHT!
SO YOU CAN STEAL PURSES FROM LI'L OLD LADIES AND MAKE A QUICK GETAWAY!

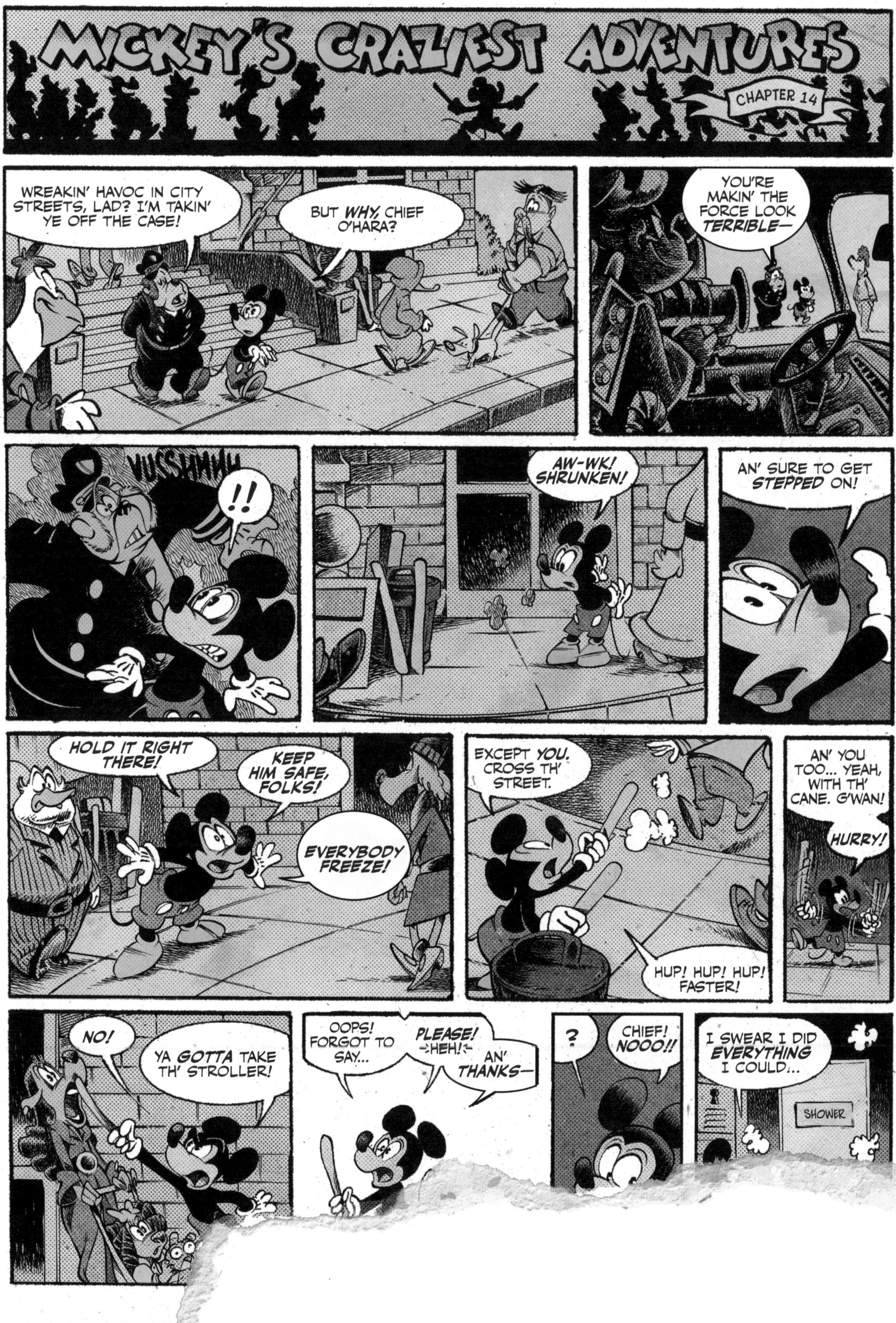
MICKEY'S CRAZIEST ADVENTURES
CHAPTER 14
WREAKIN' HAVOC IN CITY STREETS, LAD? I'M TAKIN' YE OFF THE CASE!
BUT WHY, CHIEF O'HARA?
YOU'RE MAKIN' THE FORCE LOOK TERRIBLE—
VUSSHHHH
!!
AW-WK! SHRUNKEN!
AN' SURE TO GET STEPPED ON!
HOLD IT RIGHT THERE!
KEEP HIM SAFE, FOLKS!
EVERYBODY FREEZE!
EXCEPT YOU. CROSS TH' STREET.
HUP! HUP! HUP! FASTER!
AN' YOU TOO... YEAH, WITH TH' CANE. G'WAN!
HURRY!
NO!
YA GOTTA TAKE TH' STROLLER!
OOPS! FORGOT TO SAY...
PLEASE! -HEH!-
AN' THANKS—
?
CHIEF! NOOO!!
I SWEAR I DID EVERYTHING I COULD...
SHOWER

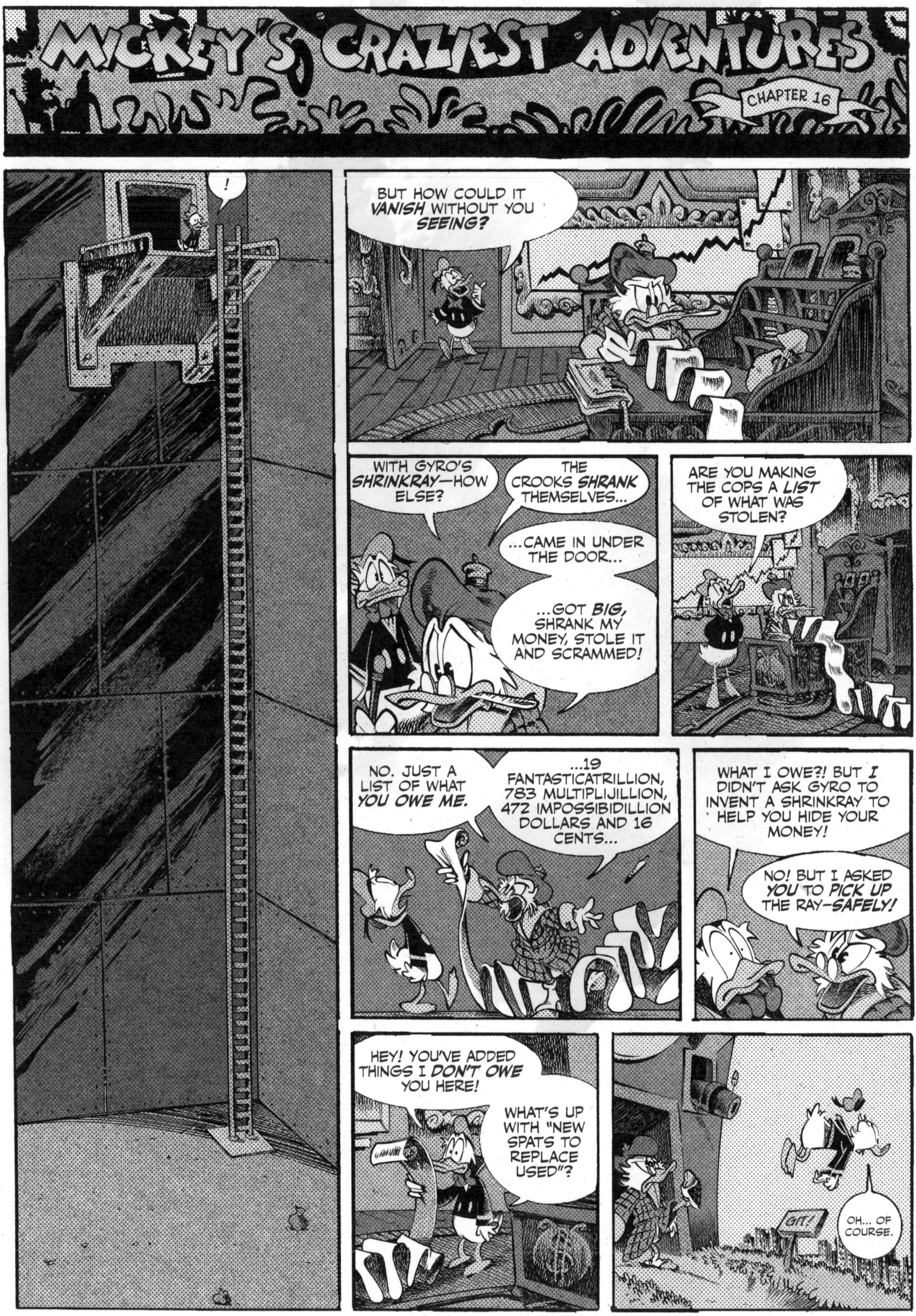
MICKEY'S CRAZIEST ADVENTURES
CHAPTER 16
!
BUT HOW COULD IT VANISH WITHOUT YOU SEEING?
WITH GYRO'S SHRINKRAY—HOW ELSE?
THE CROOKS SHRANK THEMSELVES...
...CAME IN UNDER THE DOOR...
...GOT BIG, SHRANK MY MONEY, STOLE IT AND SCRAMMED!
ARE YOU MAKING THE COPS A LIST OF WHAT WAS STOLEN?
NO. JUST A LIST OF WHAT YOU OWE ME.
...19 FANTASTICATRILLION, 783 MULTIPLIJILLION, 472 IMPOSSIBIDILLION DOLLARS AND 16 CENTS...
WHAT I OWE?! BUT I DIDN'T ASK GYRO TO INVENT A SHRINKRAY TO HELP YOU HIDE YOUR MONEY!
NO! BUT I ASKED YOU TO PICK UP THE RAY—SAFELY!
HEY! YOU'VE ADDED THINGS I DON'T OWE YOU HERE!
WHAT'S UP WITH "NEW SPATS TO REPLACE USED"?
GIT!
OH... OF COURSE.

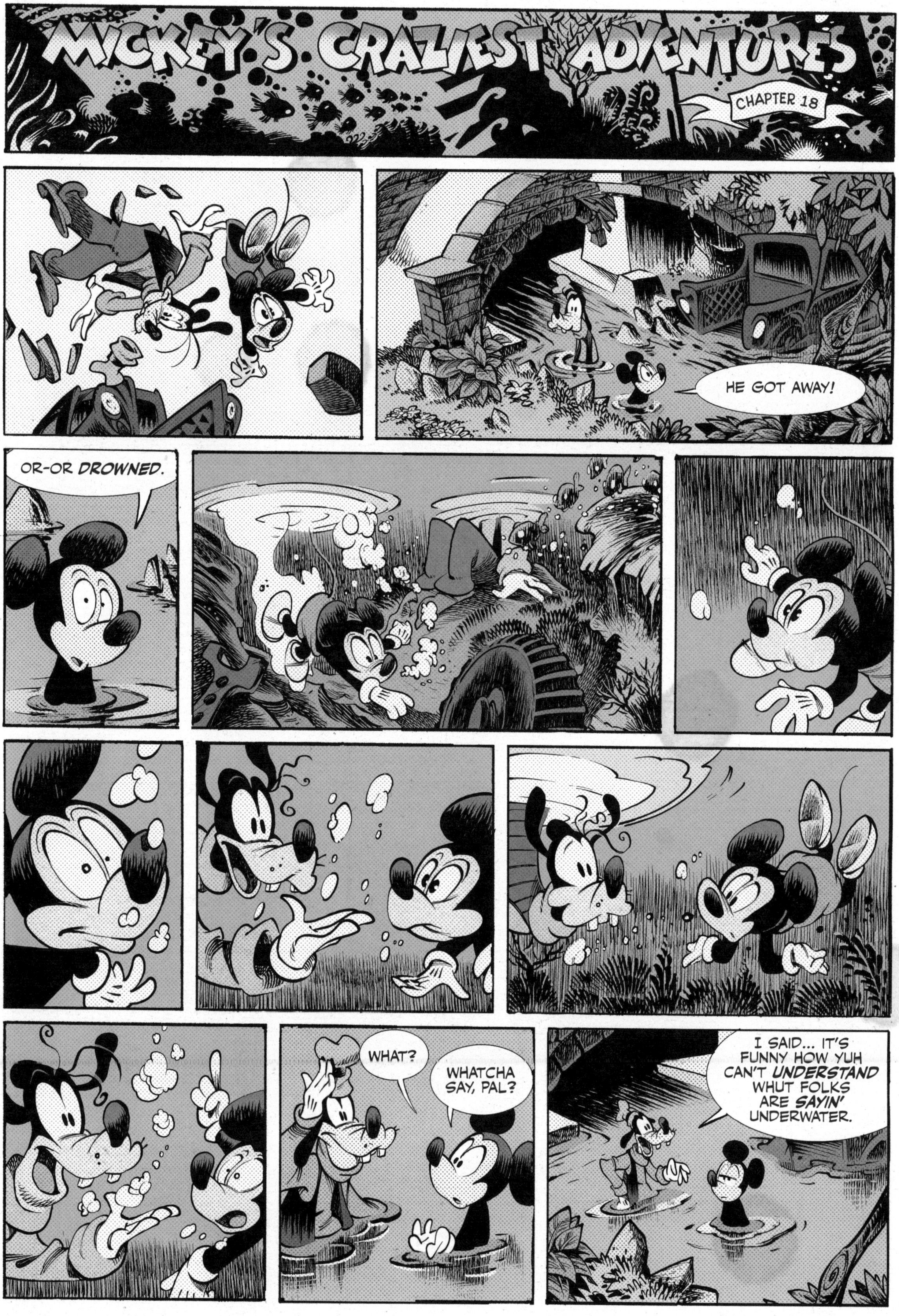
MICKEY'S CRAZIEST ADVENTURES
CHAPTER 18
HE GOT AWAY!
OR-OR DROWNED.
WHAT?
WHATCHA SAY, PAL?
I SAID... IT'S FUNNY HOW YUH CAN'T UNDERSTAND WHUT FOLKS ARE SAYIN' UNDERWATER.

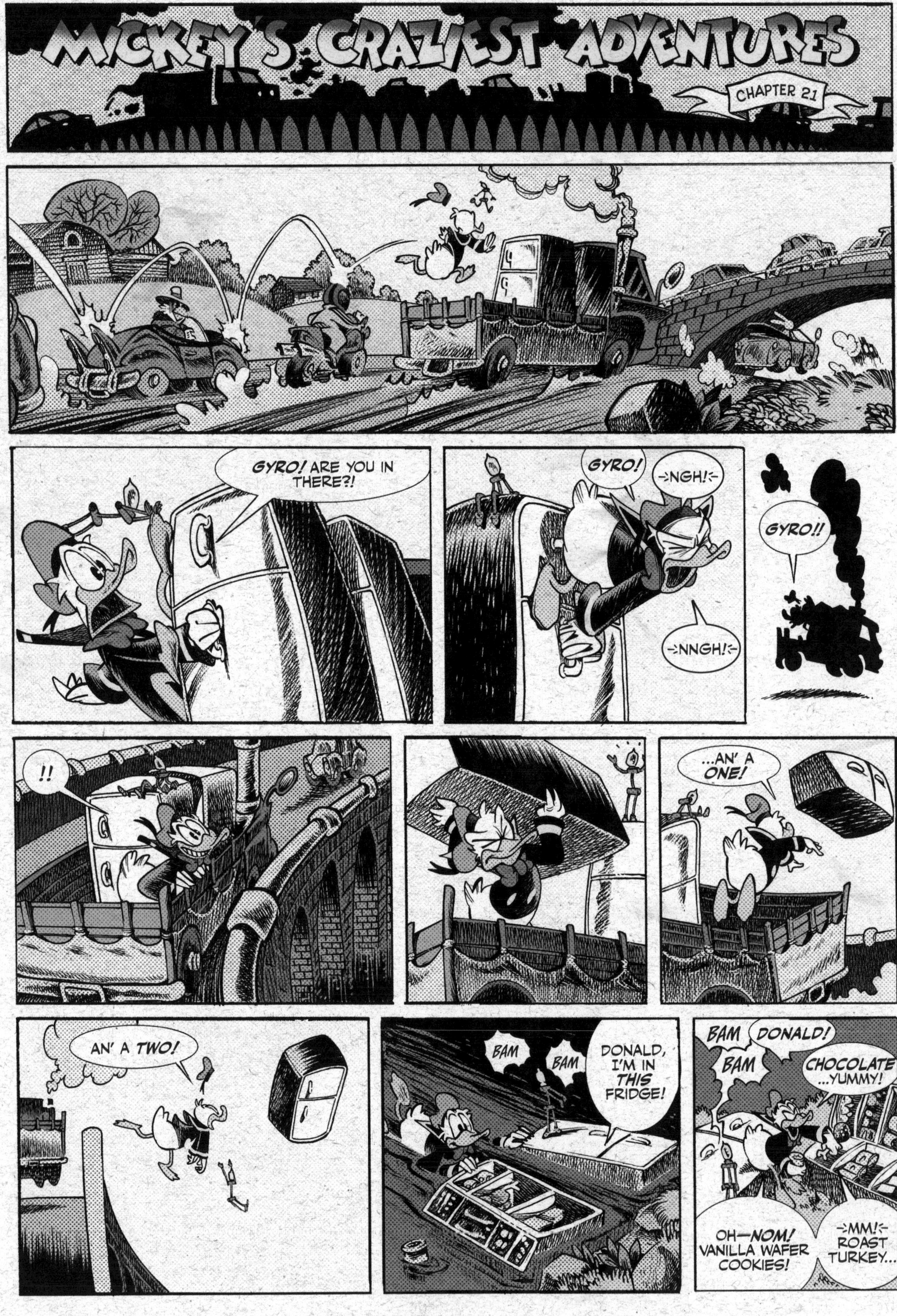
MICKEY'S CRAZIEST ADVENTURES
CHAPTER 21
GYRO! ARE YOU IN THERE?!
GYRO!
-NGH!-
-NNGH!-
GYRO!!
!!
...AN' A ONE!
AN' A TWO!
BAM
BAM
DONALD, I'M IN THIS FRIDGE!
BAM
DONALD!
BAM
CHOCOLATE ...YUMMY!
OH—NOM! VANILLA WAFER COOKIES!
-MM!- ROAST TURKEY...

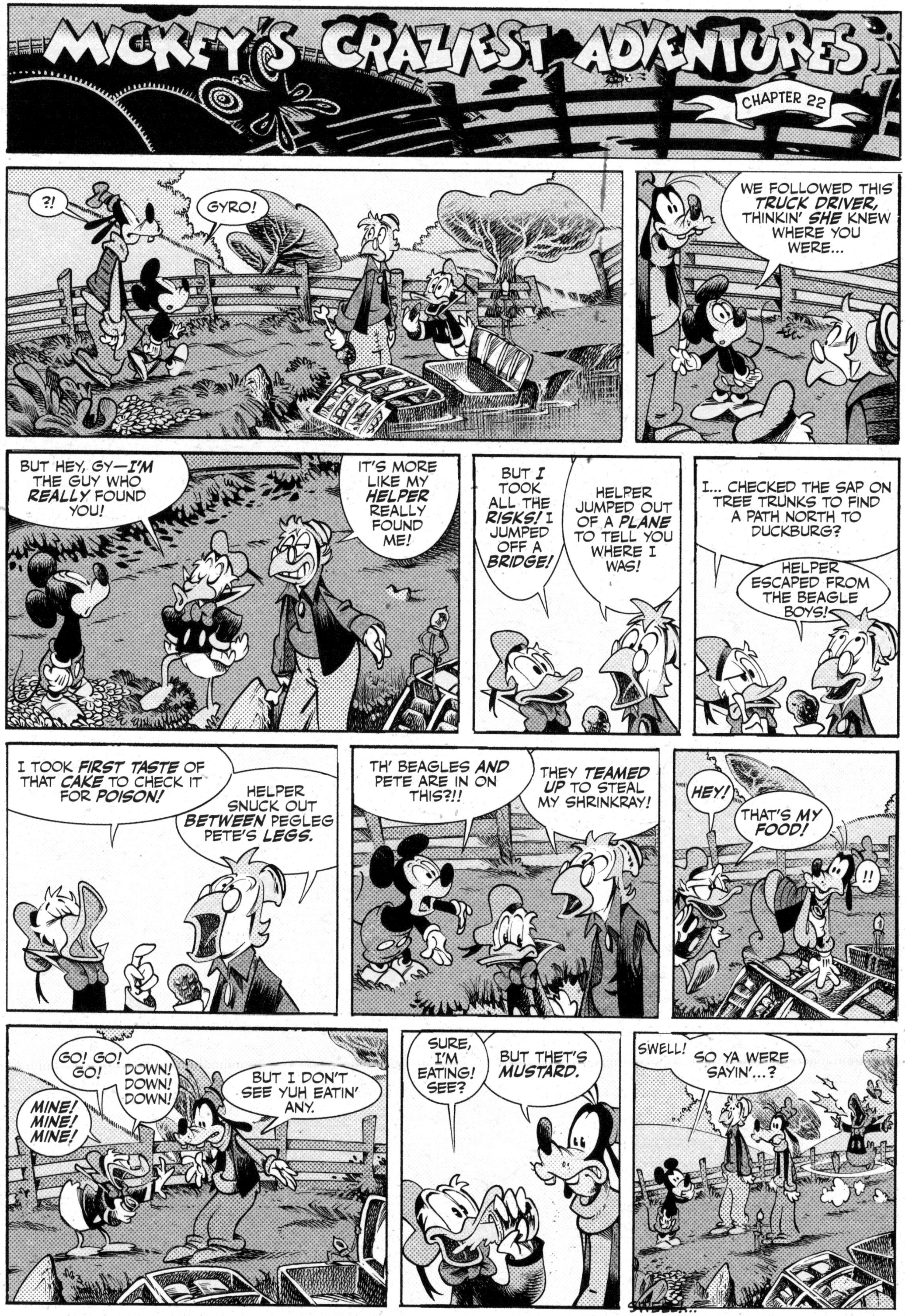
MICKEY'S CRAZIEST ADVENTURES
CHAPTER 22
?!
GYRO!
WE FOLLOWED THIS TRUCK DRIVER, THINKIN' SHE KNEW WHERE YOU WERE...
BUT HEY, GY—I'M THE GUY WHO REALLY FOUND YOU!
IT'S MORE LIKE MY HELPER REALLY FOUND ME!
BUT I TOOK ALL THE RISKS! I JUMPED OFF A BRIDGE!
HELPER JUMPED OUT OF A PLANE TO TELL YOU WHERE I WAS!
I... CHECKED THE SAP ON TREE TRUNKS TO FIND A PATH NORTH TO DUCKBURG?
HELPER ESCAPED FROM THE BEAGLE BOYS!
I TOOK FIRST TASTE OF THAT CAKE TO CHECK IT FOR POISON!
HELPER SNUCK OUT BETWEEN PEGLEG PETE'S LEGS.
TH' BEAGLES AND PETE ARE IN ON THIS?!!
THEY TEAMED UP TO STEAL MY SHRINKRAY!
HEY!
THAT'S MY FOOD!
!!
GO! GO! GO!
MINE! MINE! MINE!
DOWN! DOWN! DOWN!
BUT I DON'T SEE YUH EATIN' ANY.
SURE, I'M EATING! SEE?
BUT THET'S MUSTARD.
SWELL!
SO YA WERE SAYIN'...?

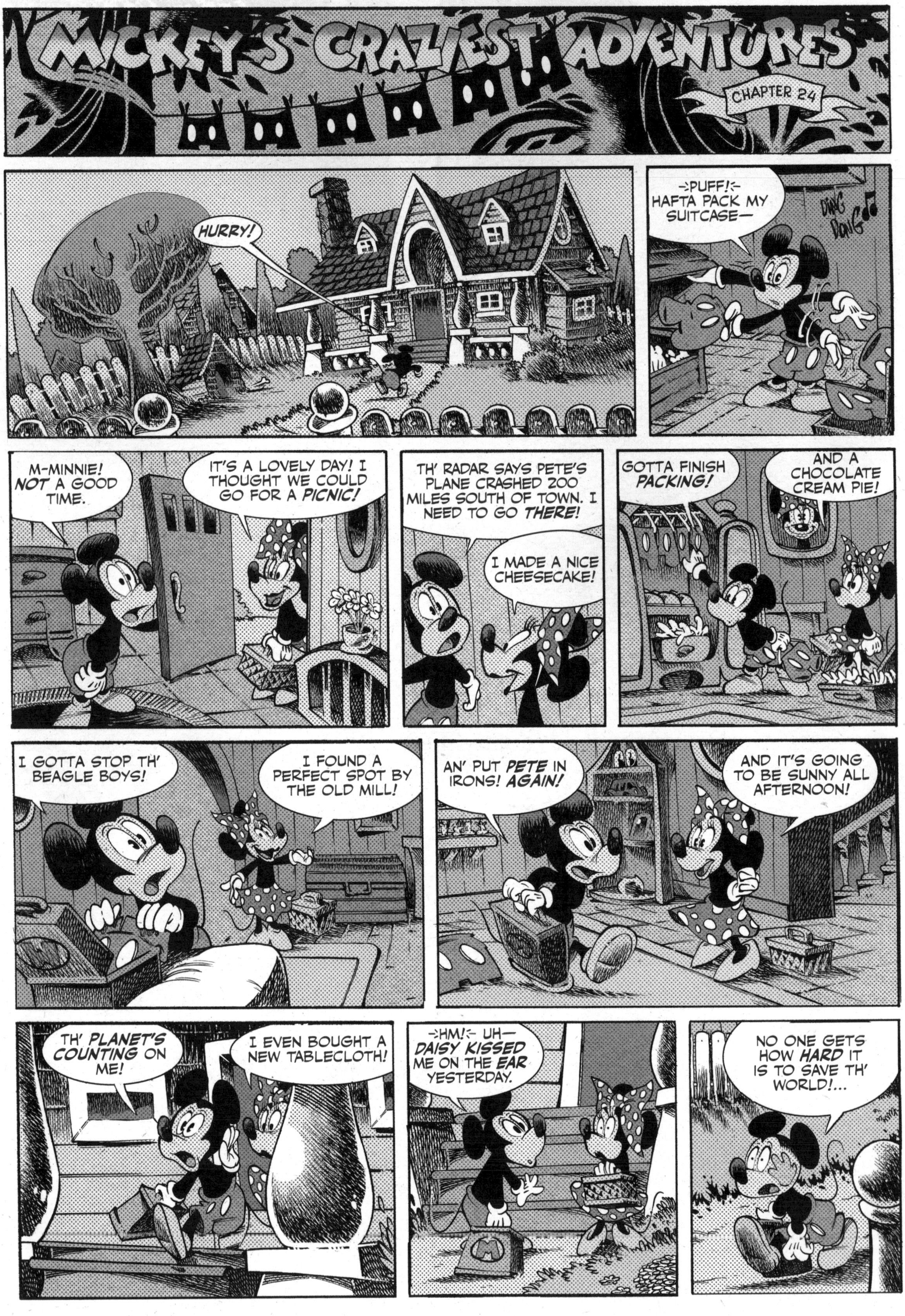
MICKEY'S CRAZIEST ADVENTURES
CHAPTER 24
HURRY!
-PUFF!- HAFTA PACK MY SUITCASE—
DING DONG
M-MINNIE! NOT A GOOD TIME.
IT'S A LOVELY DAY! I THOUGHT WE COULD GO FOR A PICNIC!
TH' RADAR SAYS PETE'S PLANE CRASHED 200 MILES SOUTH OF TOWN. I NEED TO GO THERE!
I MADE A NICE CHEESECAKE!
GOTTA FINISH PACKING!
AND A CHOCOLATE CREAM PIE!
I GOTTA STOP TH' BEAGLE BOYS!
I FOUND A PERFECT SPOT BY THE OLD MILL!
AN' PUT PETE IN IRONS! AGAIN!
AND IT'S GOING TO BE SUNNY ALL AFTERNOON!
TH' PLANET'S COUNTING ON ME!
I EVEN BOUGHT A NEW TABLECLOTH!
-HM!- UH— DAISY KISSED ME ON THE EAR YESTERDAY.
NO ONE GETS HOW HARD IT IS TO SAVE TH' WORLD!...

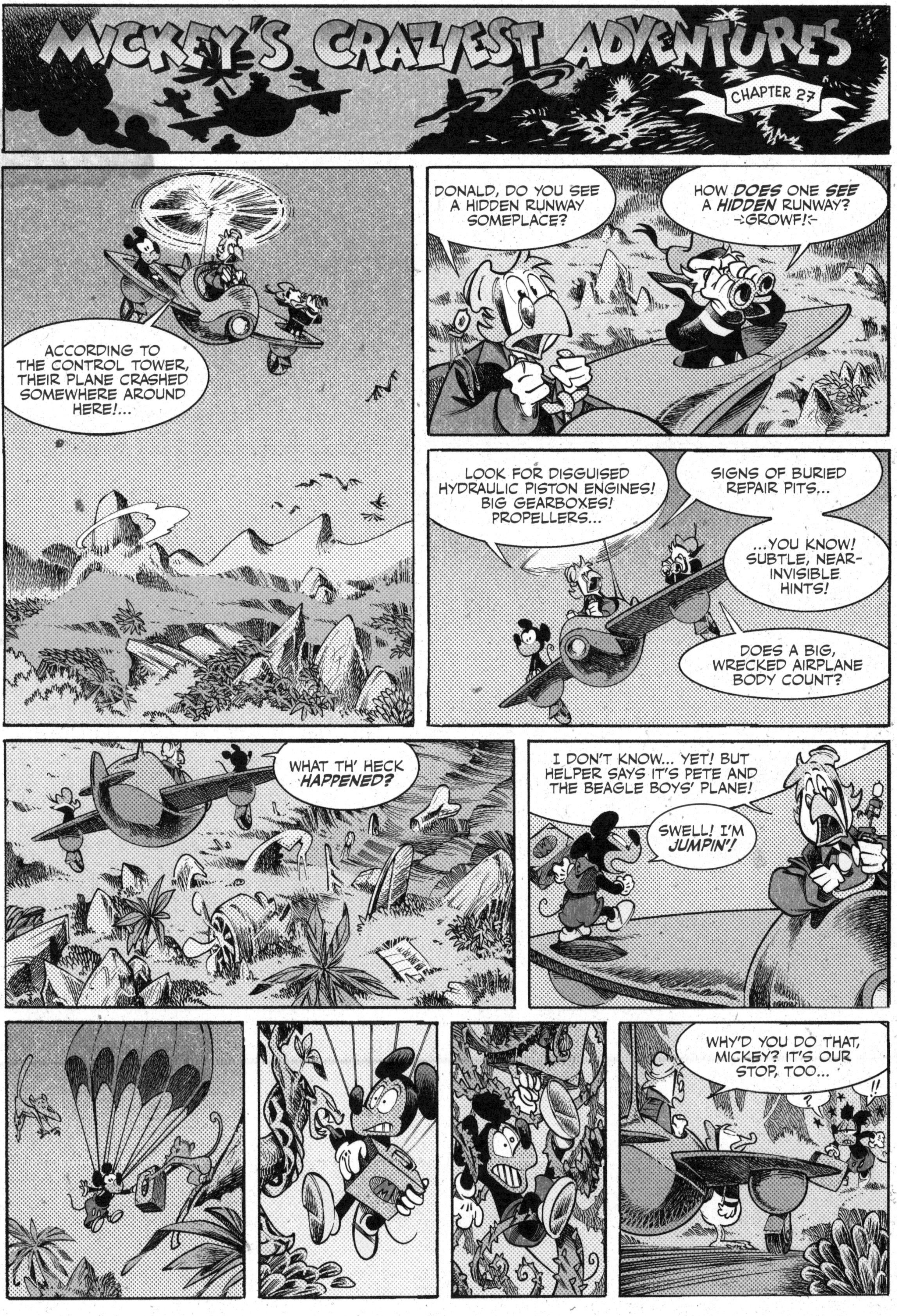
MICKEY'S CRAZIEST ADVENTURES
CHAPTER 27
ACCORDING TO THE CONTROL TOWER, THEIR PLANE CRASHED SOMEWHERE AROUND HERE!...
DONALD, DO YOU SEE A HIDDEN RUNWAY SOMEPLACE?
HOW *DOES* ONE *SEE* A *HIDDEN* RUNWAY? -GROWF!-
LOOK FOR DISGUISED HYDRAULIC PISTON ENGINES! BIG GEARBOXES! PROPELLERS...
SIGNS OF BURIED REPAIR PITS...
...YOU KNOW! SUBTLE, NEAR-INVISIBLE HINTS!
DOES A BIG, WRECKED AIRPLANE BODY COUNT?
WHAT TH' HECK *HAPPENED?*
I DON'T KNOW... YET! BUT HELPER SAYS IT'S PETE AND THE BEAGLE BOYS' PLANE!
SWELL! I'M *JUMPIN'!*
WHY'D YOU DO THAT, MICKEY? IT'S OUR STOP, TOO...
?
!!

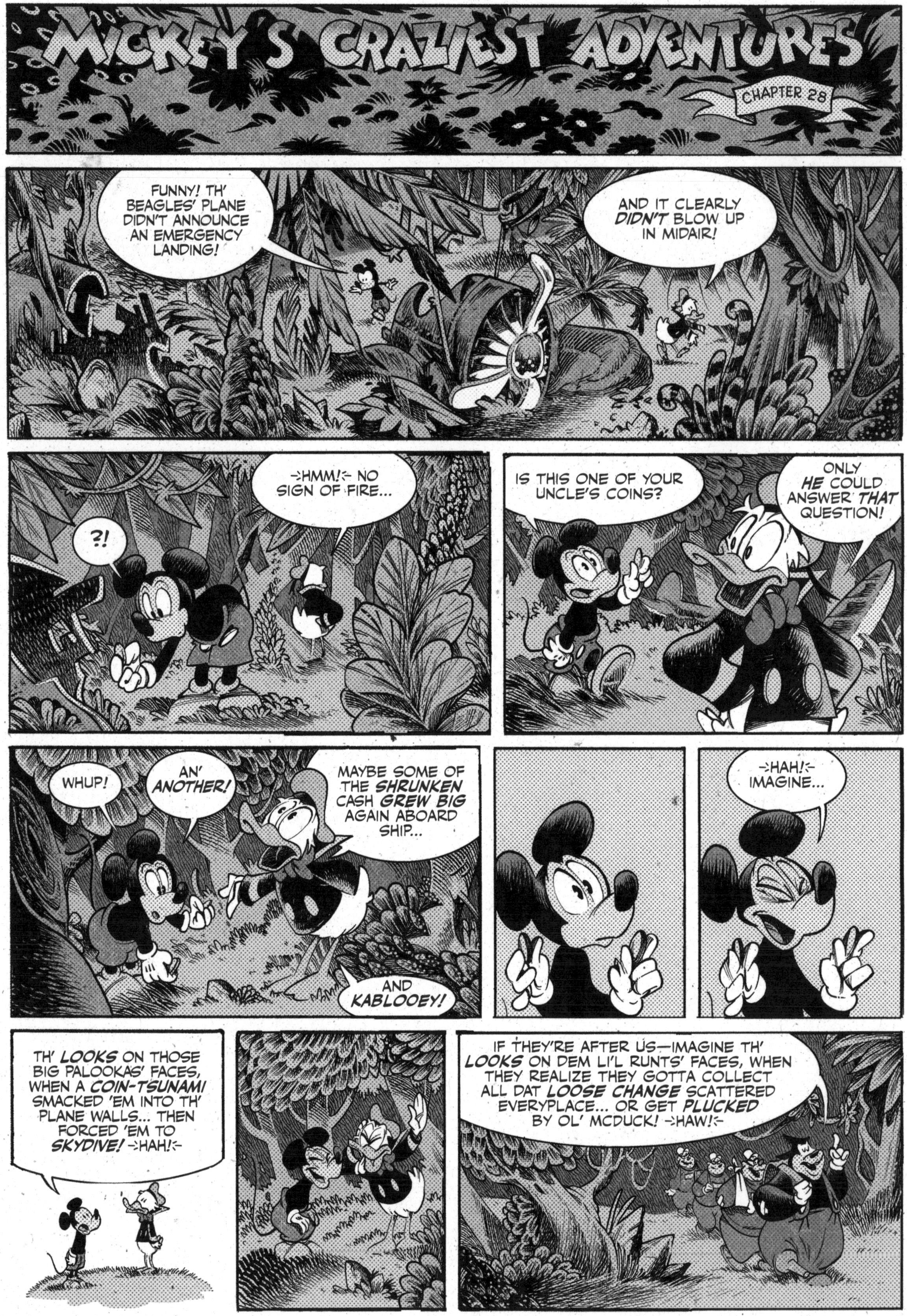

MICKEY'S CRAZIEST ADVENTURES
CHAPTER 28
FUNNY! TH' BEAGLES' PLANE DIDN'T ANNOUNCE AN EMERGENCY LANDING!
AND IT CLEARLY DIDN'T BLOW UP IN MIDAIR!
?!
-HMM!- NO SIGN OF FIRE...
IS THIS ONE OF YOUR UNCLE'S COINS?
ONLY HE COULD ANSWER THAT QUESTION!
WHUP!
AN' ANOTHER!
MAYBE SOME OF THE SHRUNKEN CASH GREW BIG AGAIN ABOARD SHIP...
AND KABLOOEY!
-HAH!- IMAGINE...
TH' LOOKS ON THOSE BIG PALOOKAS' FACES, WHEN A COIN-TSUNAMI SMACKED 'EM INTO TH' PLANE WALLS... THEN FORCED 'EM TO SKYDIVE! -HAH!-
IF THEY'RE AFTER US—IMAGINE TH' LOOKS ON DEM LI'L RUNTS' FACES, WHEN THEY REALIZE THEY GOTTA COLLECT ALL DAT LOOSE CHANGE SCATTERED EVERYPLACE... OR GET PLUCKED BY OL' MCDUCK! -HAW!-

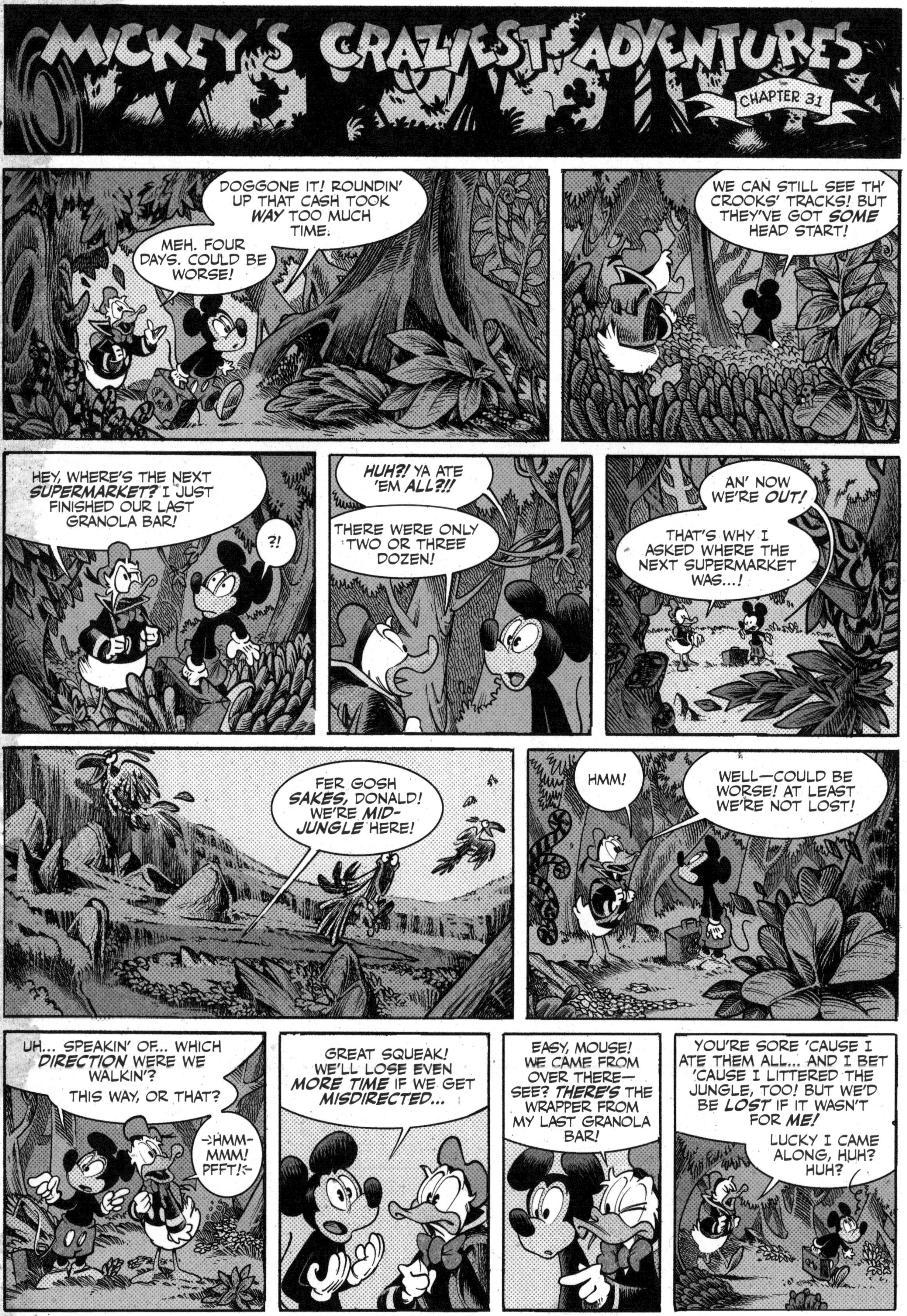
MICKEY'S CRAZIEST ADVENTURES
CHAPTER 31
DOGGONE IT! ROUNDIN' UP THAT CASH TOOK WAY TOO MUCH TIME.
MEH. FOUR DAYS. COULD BE WORSE!
WE CAN STILL SEE TH' CROOKS' TRACKS! BUT THEY'VE GOT SOME HEAD START!
HEY, WHERE'S THE NEXT SUPERMARKET? I JUST FINISHED OUR LAST GRANOLA BAR!
?!
HUH?! YA ATE 'EM ALL?!!
THERE WERE ONLY TWO OR THREE DOZEN!
AN' NOW WE'RE OUT!
THAT'S WHY I ASKED WHERE THE NEXT SUPERMARKET WAS...!
FER GOSH SAKES, DONALD! WE'RE MID-JUNGLE HERE!
HMM!
WELL—COULD BE WORSE! AT LEAST WE'RE NOT LOST!
UH... SPEAKIN' OF... WHICH DIRECTION WERE WE WALKIN'?
THIS WAY, OR THAT?
HMM-MMM! PFFT!
GREAT SQUEAK! WE'LL LOSE EVEN MORE TIME IF WE GET MISDIRECTED...
EASY, MOUSE! WE CAME FROM OVER THERE— SEE? THERE'S THE WRAPPER FROM MY LAST GRANOLA BAR!
YOU'RE SORE 'CAUSE I ATE THEM ALL... AND I BET 'CAUSE I LITTERED THE JUNGLE, TOO! BUT WE'D BE LOST IF IT WASN'T FOR ME!
LUCKY I CAME ALONG, HUH? HUH?

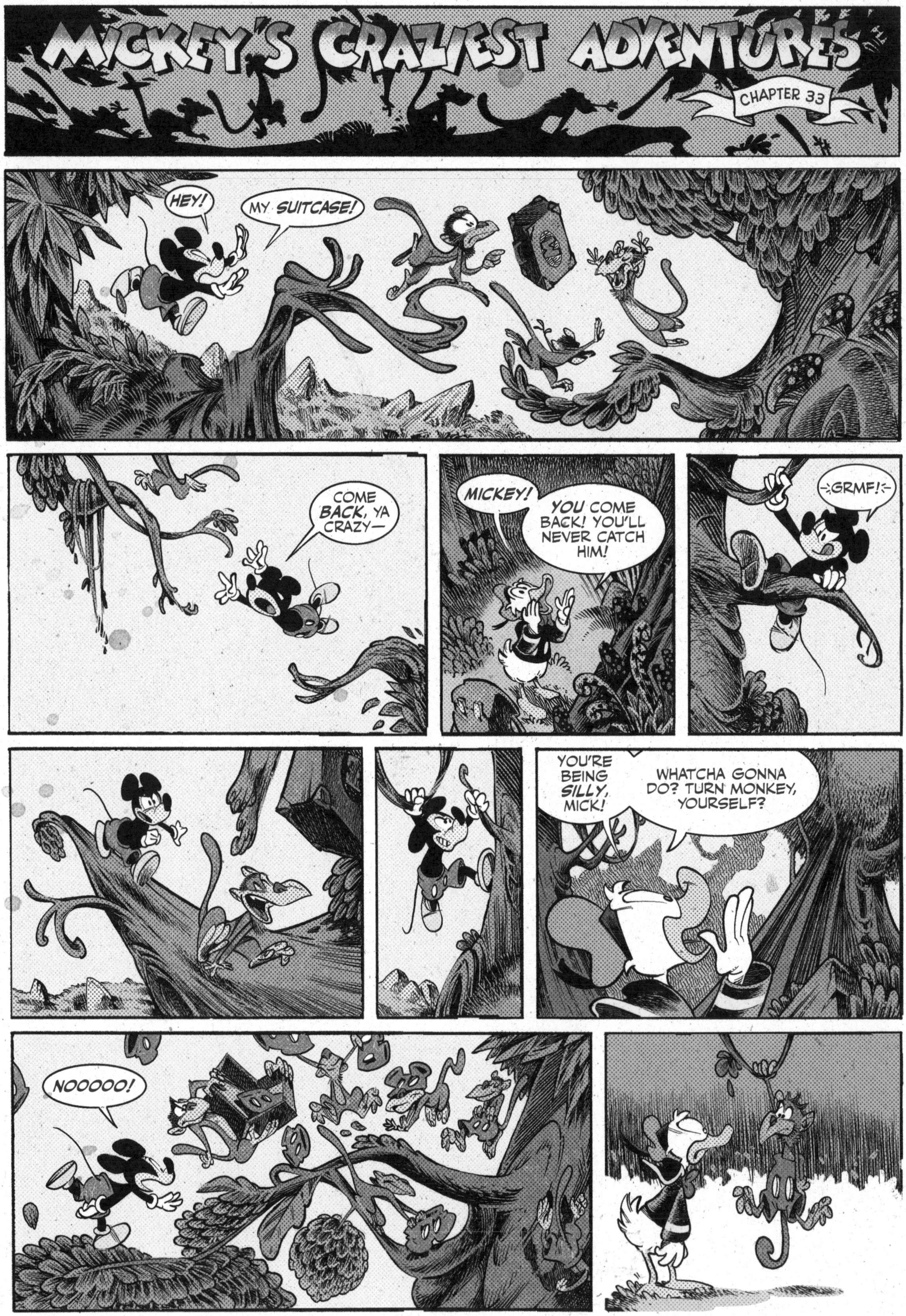
MICKEY'S CRAZIEST ADVENTURES
CHAPTER 33
HEY!
MY SUITCASE!
COME BACK, YA CRAZY—
MICKEY!
YOU COME BACK! YOU'LL NEVER CATCH HIM!
GRMF!
YOU'RE BEING SILLY, MICK!
WHATCHA GONNA DO? TURN MONKEY, YOURSELF?
NOOOOO!

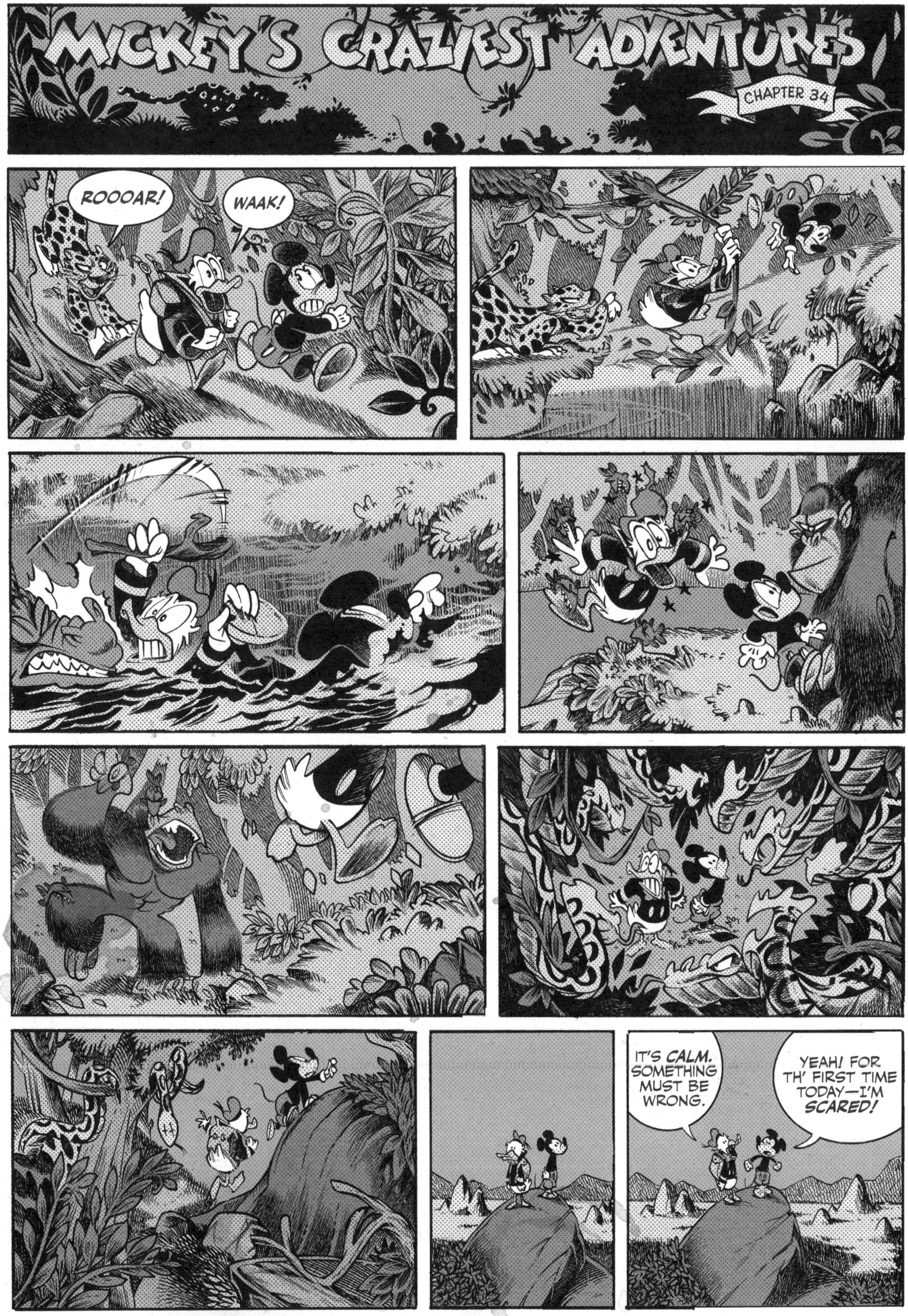
MICKEY'S CRAZIEST ADVENTURES
CHAPTER 34
ROOOAR!
WAAK!
IT'S CALM. SOMETHING MUST BE WRONG.
YEAH! FOR TH' FIRST TIME TODAY—I'M SCARED!

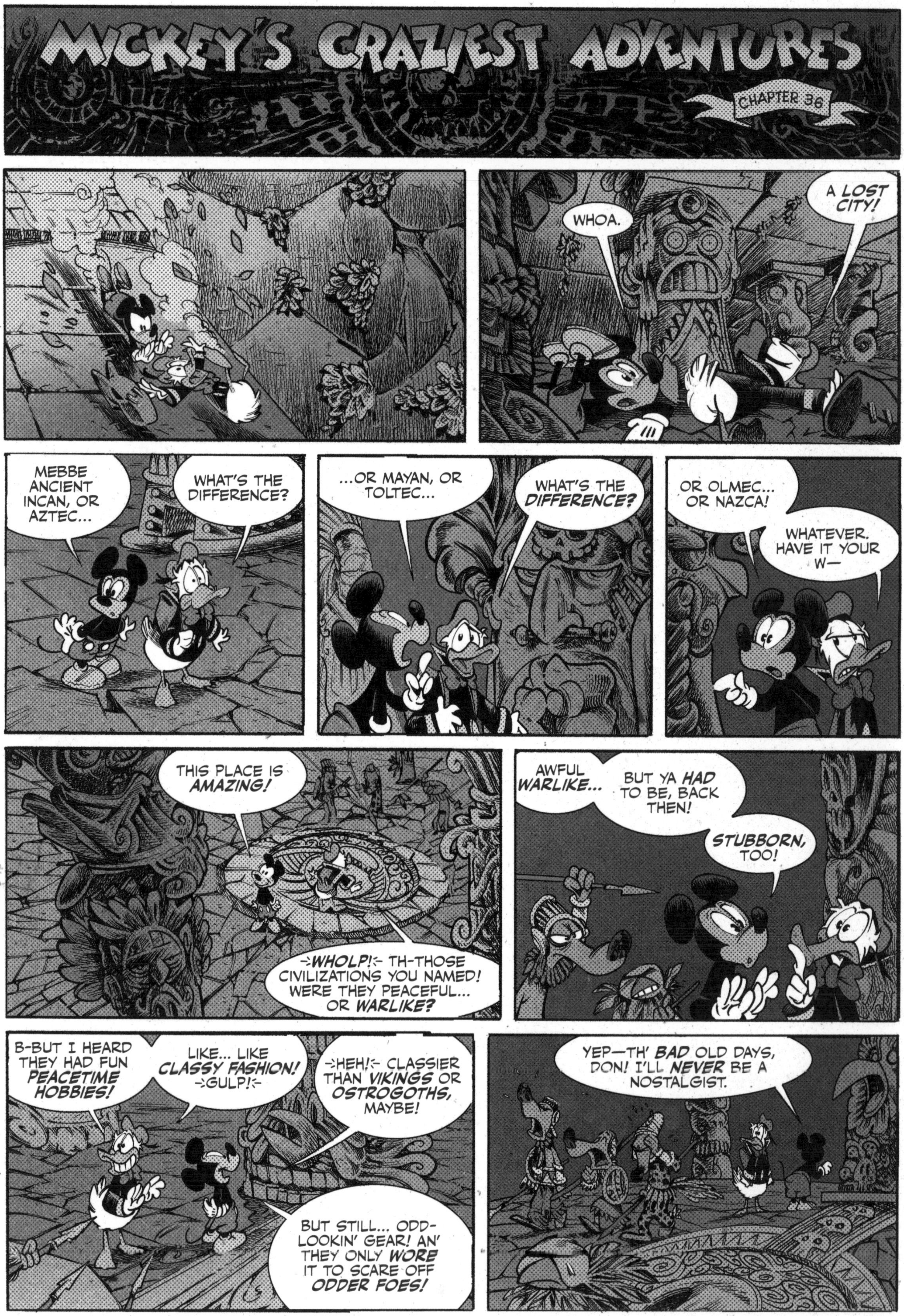
MICKEY'S CRAZIEST ADVENTURES
CHAPTER 36
WHOA.
A LOST CITY!
MEBBE ANCIENT INCAN, OR AZTEC...
WHAT'S THE DIFFERENCE?
...OR MAYAN, OR TOLTEC...
WHAT'S THE DIFFERENCE?
OR OLMEC... OR NAZCA!
WHATEVER. HAVE IT YOUR W—
THIS PLACE IS AMAZING!
-WHOLP!- TH-THOSE CIVILIZATIONS YOU NAMED! WERE THEY PEACEFUL... OR WARLIKE?
AWFUL WARLIKE...
BUT YA HAD TO BE, BACK THEN!
STUBBORN, TOO!
B-BUT I HEARD THEY HAD FUN PEACETIME HOBBIES!
LIKE... LIKE CLASSY FASHION! -GULP!-
-HEH!- CLASSIER THAN VIKINGS OR OSTROGOTHS, MAYBE!
BUT STILL... ODD-LOOKIN' GEAR! AN' THEY ONLY WORE IT TO SCARE OFF ODDER FOES!
YEP—TH' BAD OLD DAYS, DON! I'LL NEVER BE A NOSTALGIST.

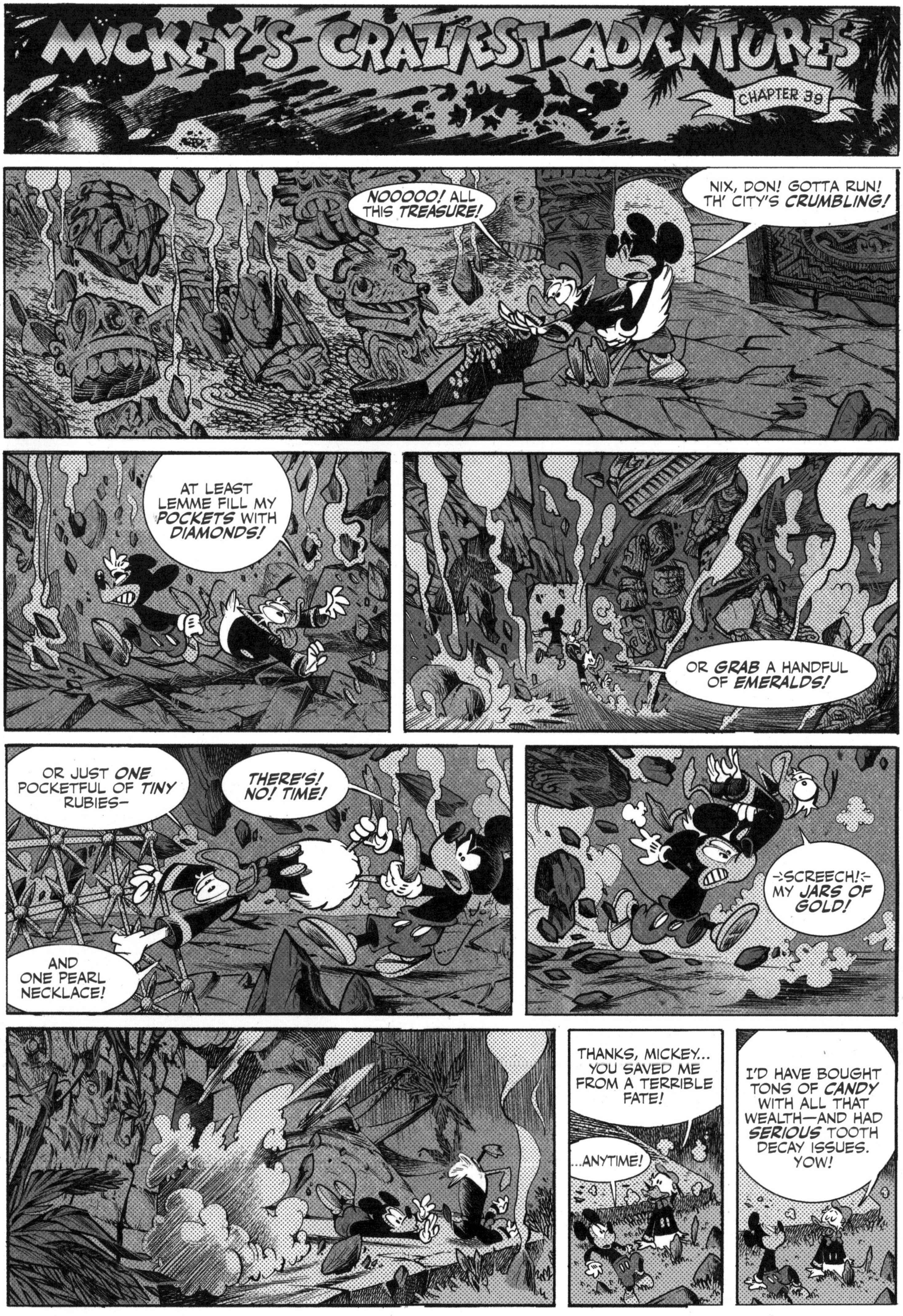
MICKEY'S CRAZIEST ADVENTURES
CHAPTER 39
NOOOOO! ALL THIS TREASURE!
NIX, DON! GOTTA RUN! TH' CITY'S CRUMBLING!
AT LEAST LEMME FILL MY POCKETS WITH DIAMONDS!
OR GRAB A HANDFUL OF EMERALDS!
OR JUST ONE POCKETFUL OF TINY RUBIES—
THERE'S! NO! TIME!
AND ONE PEARL NECKLACE!
SCREECH! MY JARS OF GOLD!
THANKS, MICKEY... YOU SAVED ME FROM A TERRIBLE FATE!
...ANYTIME!
I'D HAVE BOUGHT TONS OF CANDY WITH ALL THAT WEALTH—AND HAD SERIOUS TOOTH DECAY ISSUES. YOW!

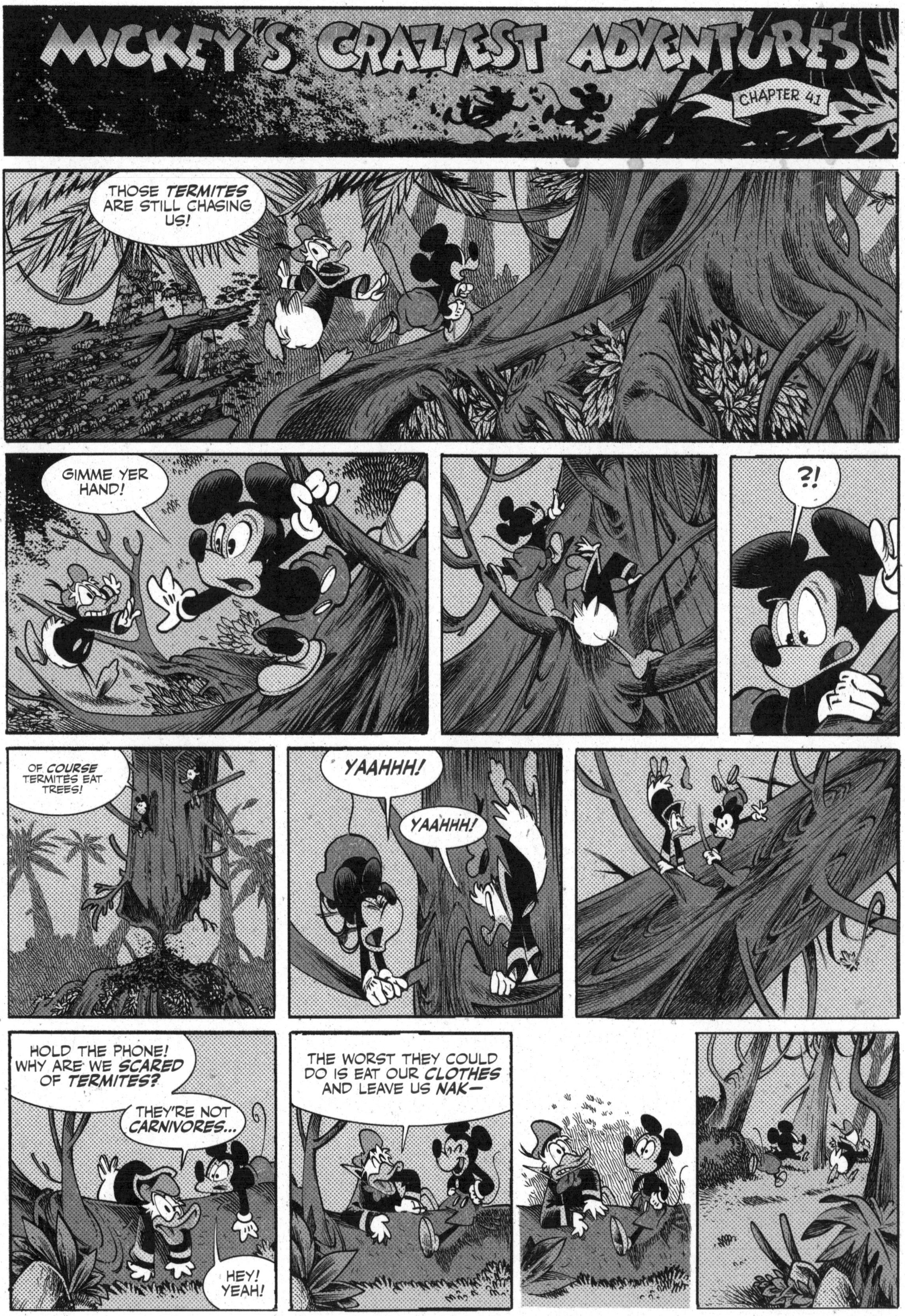
MICKEY'S CRAZIEST ADVENTURES
CHAPTER 41
THOSE TERMITES ARE STILL CHASING US!
GIMME YER HAND!
?!
OF COURSE TERMITES EAT TREES!
YAAHHH!
YAAHHH!
HOLD THE PHONE! WHY ARE WE SCARED OF TERMITES?
THEY'RE NOT CARNIVORES...
HEY! YEAH!
THE WORST THEY COULD DO IS EAT OUR CLOTHES AND LEAVE US NAK—

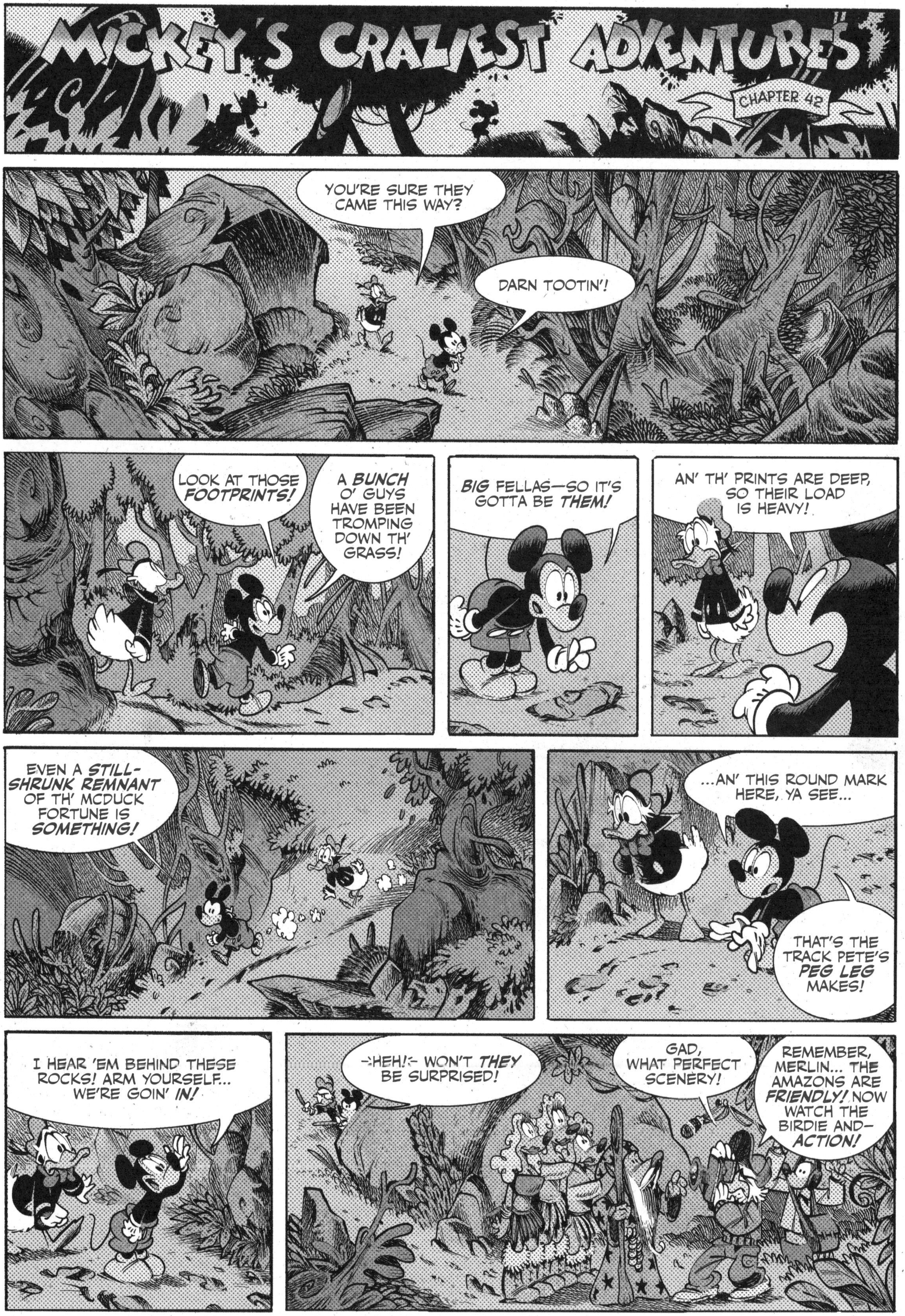
MICKEY'S CRAZIEST ADVENTURES
CHAPTER 42
YOU'RE SURE THEY CAME THIS WAY?
DARN TOOTIN'!
LOOK AT THOSE FOOTPRINTS!
A BUNCH O' GUYS HAVE BEEN TROMPING DOWN TH' GRASS!
BIG FELLAS—SO IT'S GOTTA BE THEM!
AN' TH' PRINTS ARE DEEP, SO THEIR LOAD IS HEAVY!
EVEN A STILL-SHRUNK REMNANT OF TH' MCDUCK FORTUNE IS SOMETHING!
...AN' THIS ROUND MARK HERE, YA SEE...
THAT'S THE TRACK PETE'S PEG LEG MAKES!
I HEAR 'EM BEHIND THESE ROCKS! ARM YOURSELF... WE'RE GOIN' IN!
-HEH!- WON'T THEY BE SURPRISED!
GAD, WHAT PERFECT SCENERY!
REMEMBER, MERLIN... THE AMAZONS ARE FRIENDLY! NOW WATCH THE BIRDIE AND—ACTION!

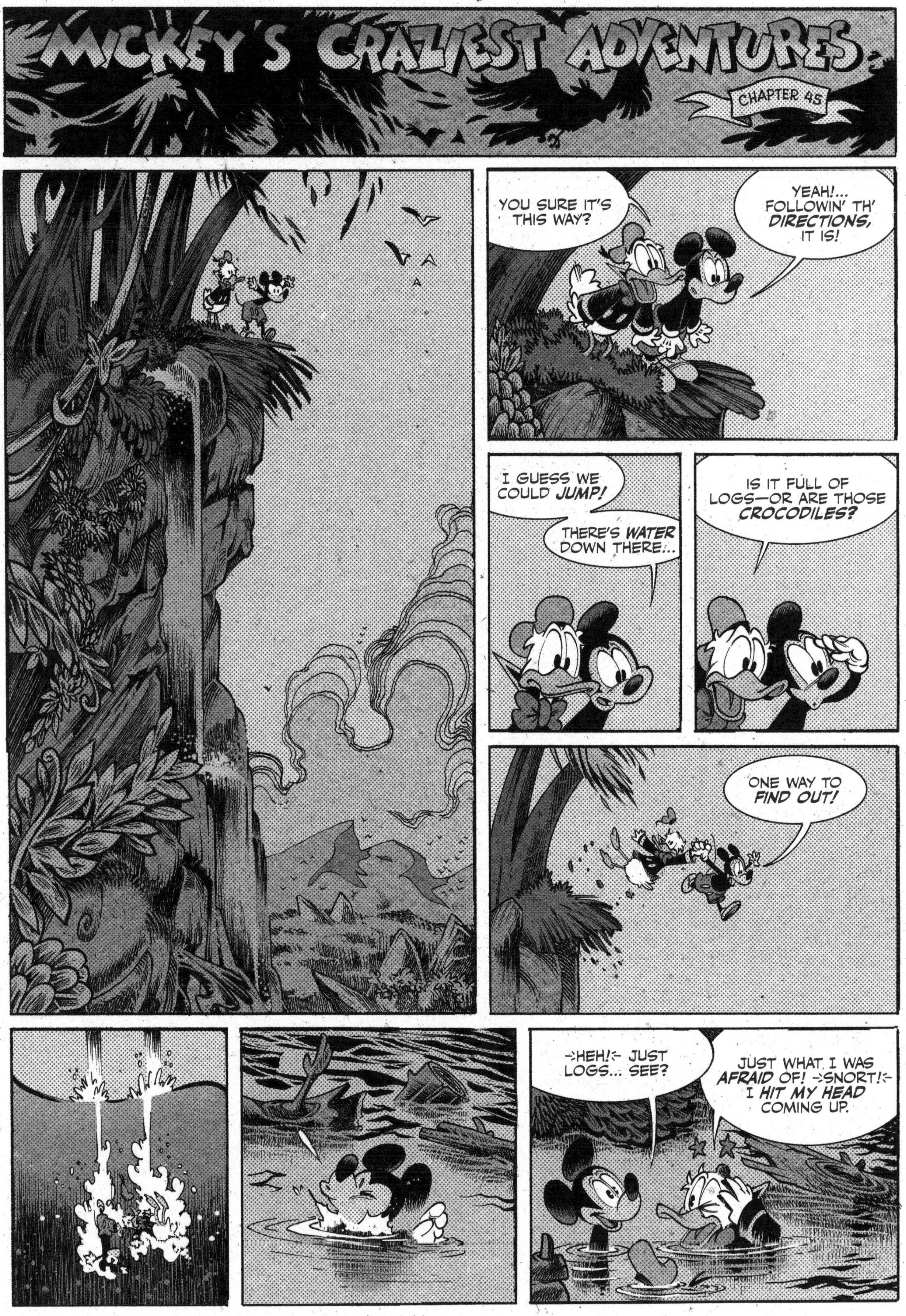
MICKEY'S CRAZIEST ADVENTURES
CHAPTER 45
YOU SURE IT'S THIS WAY?
YEAH!... FOLLOWIN' TH' DIRECTIONS, IT IS!
I GUESS WE COULD JUMP!
THERE'S WATER DOWN THERE...
IS IT FULL OF LOGS—OR ARE THOSE CROCODILES?
ONE WAY TO FIND OUT!
-HEH!- JUST LOGS... SEE?
JUST WHAT I WAS AFRAID OF! -SNORT!- I HIT MY HEAD COMING UP.

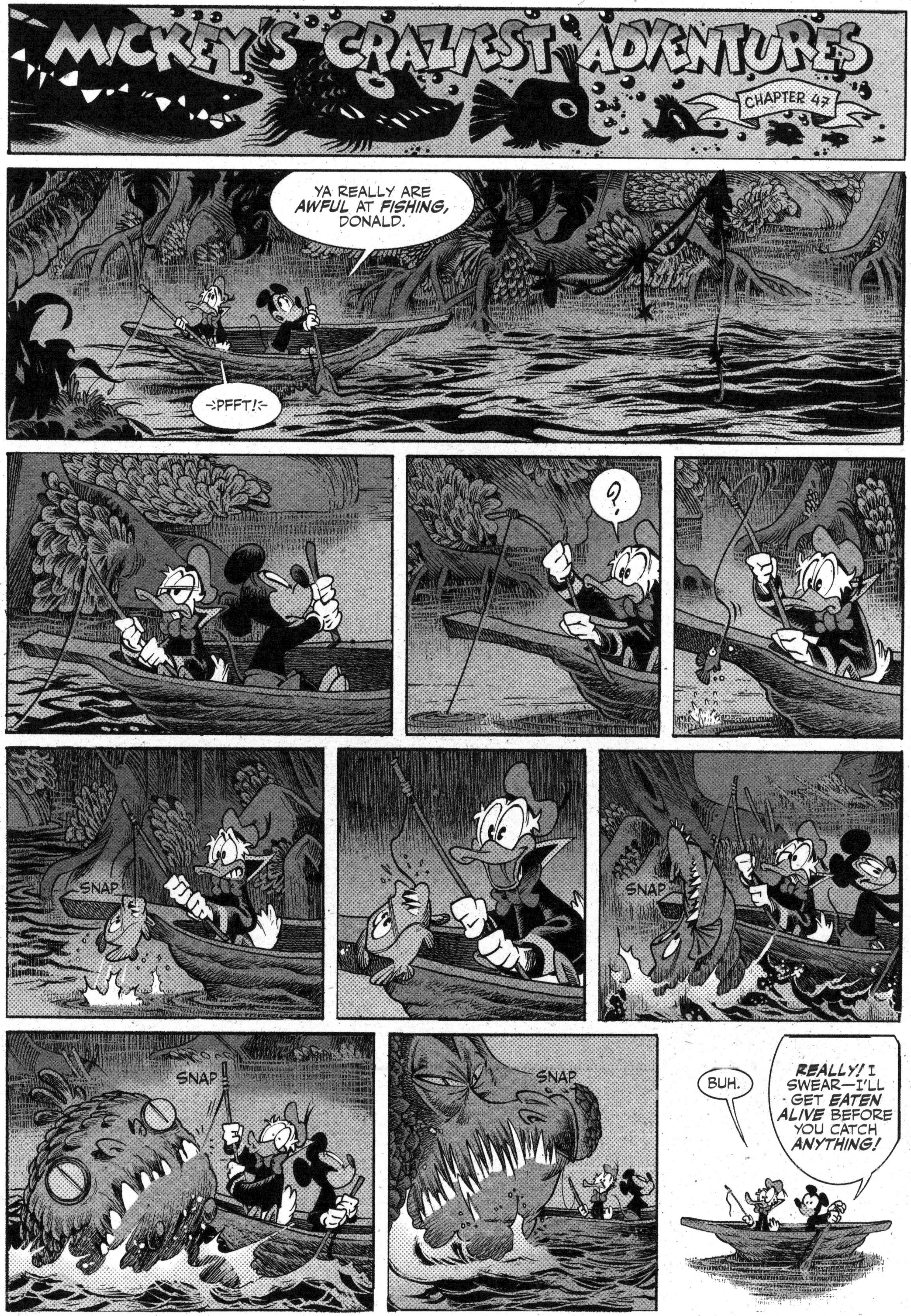
MICKEY'S CRAZIEST ADVENTURES
CHAPTER 47
YA REALLY ARE AWFUL AT FISHING, DONALD.
PFFT!
?
SNAP
SNAP
SNAP
SNAP
BUH.
REALLY! I SWEAR—I'LL GET EATEN ALIVE BEFORE YOU CATCH ANYTHING!

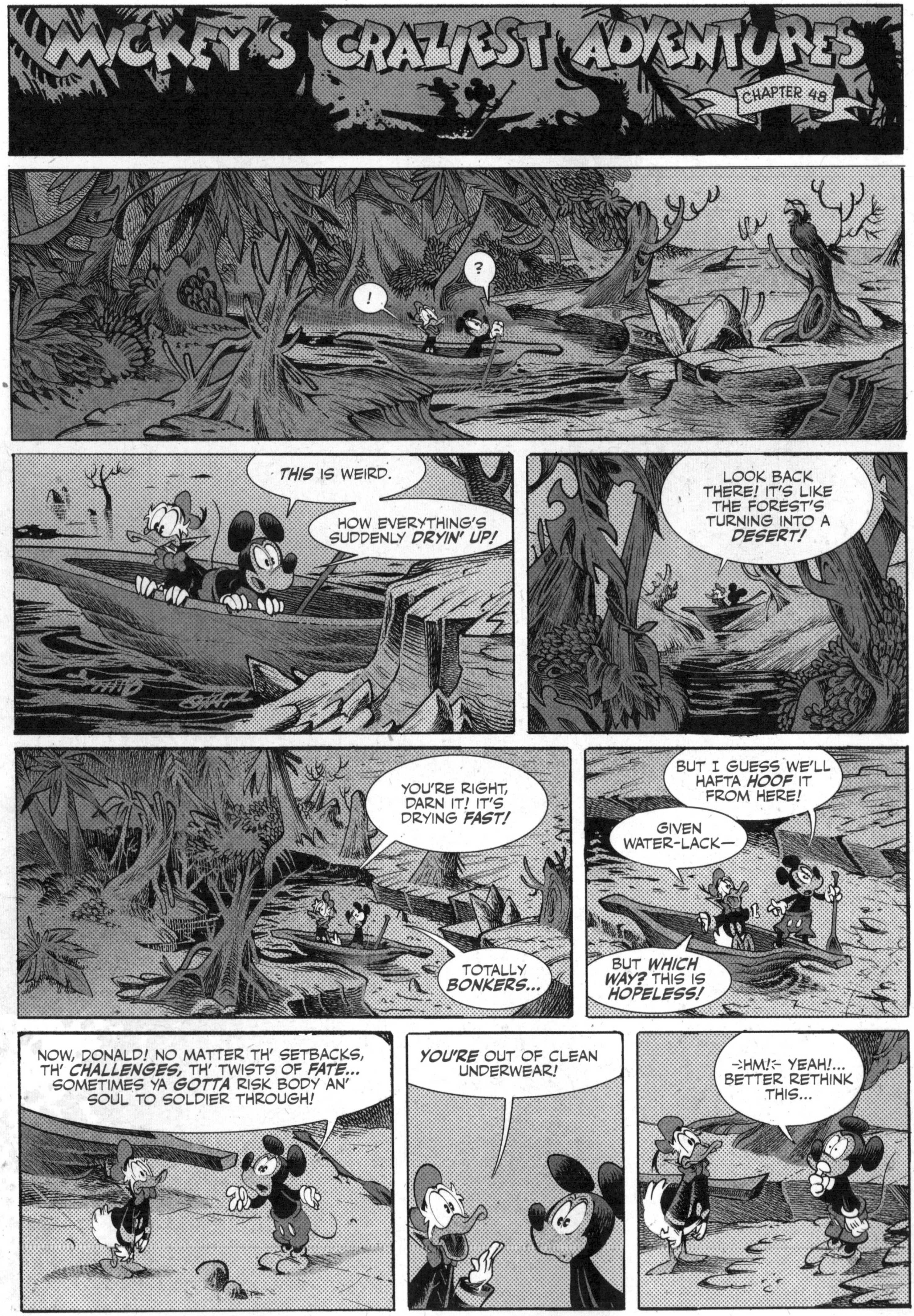
MICKEY'S CRAZIEST ADVENTURES
CHAPTER 48
!
?
THIS IS WEIRD.
HOW EVERYTHING'S SUDDENLY DRYIN' UP!
LOOK BACK THERE! IT'S LIKE THE FOREST'S TURNING INTO A DESERT!
YOU'RE RIGHT, DARN IT! IT'S DRYING FAST!
TOTALLY BONKERS...
BUT I GUESS WE'LL HAFTA HOOF IT FROM HERE!
GIVEN WATER-LACK—
BUT WHICH WAY? THIS IS HOPELESS!
NOW, DONALD! NO MATTER TH' SETBACKS, TH' CHALLENGES, TH' TWISTS OF FATE... SOMETIMES YA GOTTA RISK BODY AN' SOUL TO SOLDIER THROUGH!
YOU'RE OUT OF CLEAN UNDERWEAR!
HM! YEAH!... BETTER RETHINK THIS...

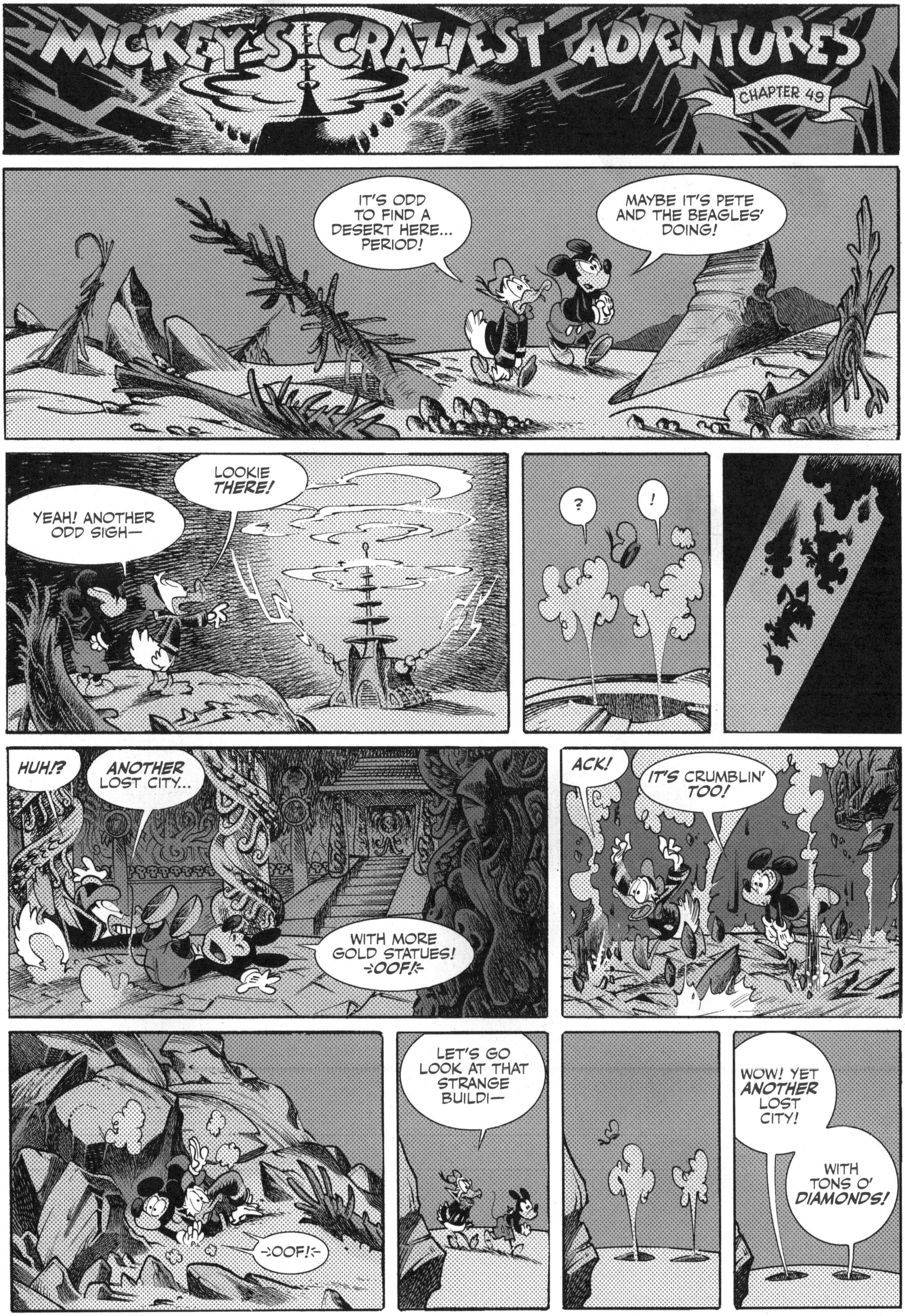
MICKEY'S CRAZIEST ADVENTURES
CHAPTER 49
IT'S ODD TO FIND A DESERT HERE... PERIOD!
MAYBE IT'S PETE AND THE BEAGLES' DOING!
LOOKIE THERE!
YEAH! ANOTHER ODD SIGH—
?
!
HUH!?
ANOTHER LOST CITY...
WITH MORE GOLD STATUES! -OOF!-
ACK!
IT'S CRUMBLIN' TOO!
-OOF!-
LET'S GO LOOK AT THAT STRANGE BUILDI—
WOW! YET ANOTHER LOST CITY!
WITH TONS O' DIAMONDS!

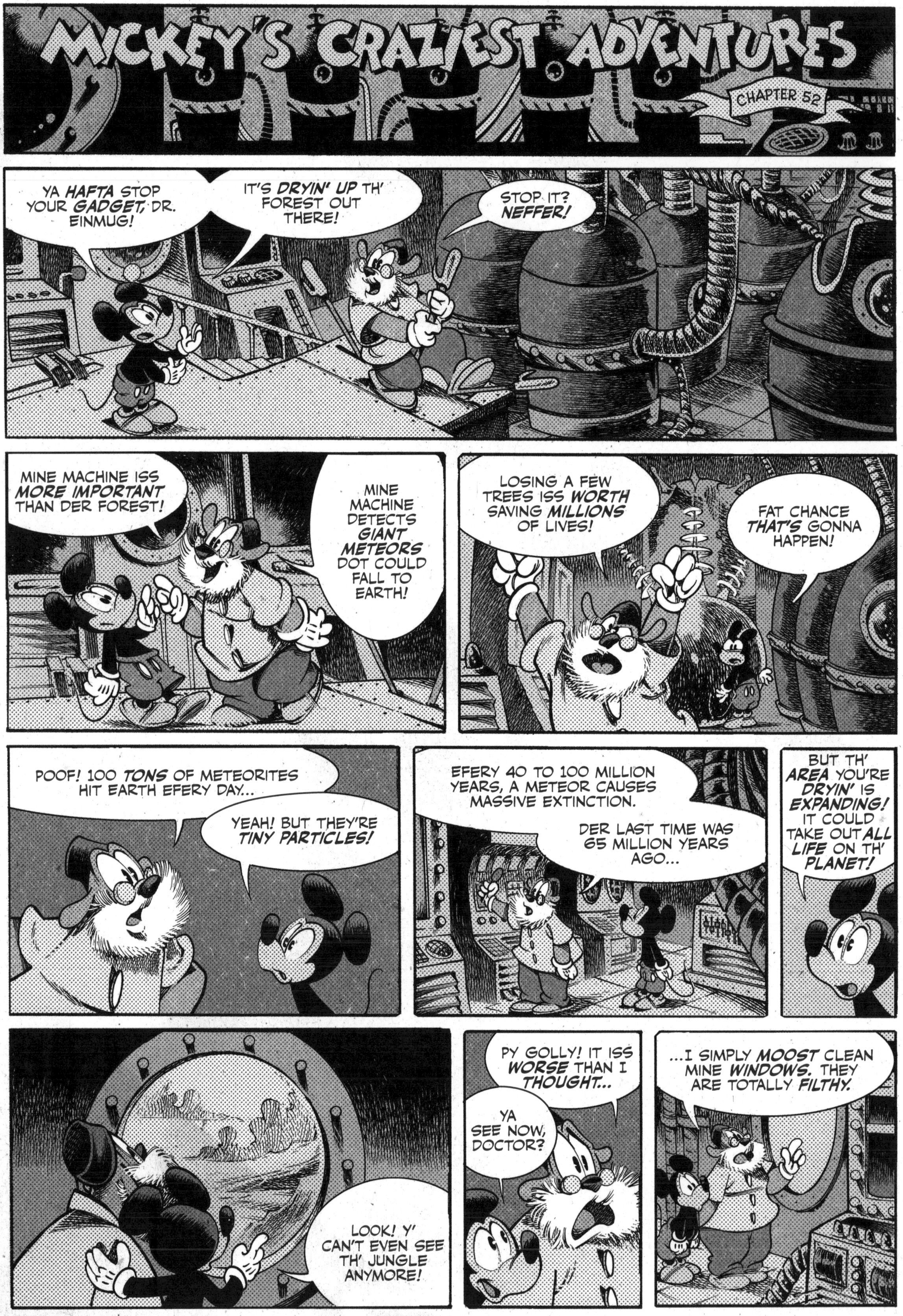
MICKEY'S CRAZIEST ADVENTURES
CHAPTER 52
YA HAFTA STOP YOUR GADGET, DR. EINMUG!
IT'S DRYIN' UP TH' FOREST OUT THERE!
STOP IT? NEFFER!
MINE MACHINE ISS MORE IMPORTANT THAN DER FOREST!
MINE MACHINE DETECTS GIANT METEORS DOT COULD FALL TO EARTH!
LOSING A FEW TREES ISS WORTH SAVING MILLIONS OF LIVES!
FAT CHANCE THAT'S GONNA HAPPEN!
POOF! 100 TONS OF METEORITES HIT EARTH EFERY DAY...
YEAH! BUT THEY'RE TINY PARTICLES!
EFERY 40 TO 100 MILLION YEARS, A METEOR CAUSES MASSIVE EXTINCTION.
DER LAST TIME WAS 65 MILLION YEARS AGO...
BUT TH' AREA YOU'RE DRYIN' IS EXPANDING! IT COULD TAKE OUT ALL LIFE ON TH' PLANET!
LOOK! Y' CAN'T EVEN SEE TH' JUNGLE ANYMORE!
PY GOLLY! IT ISS WORSE THAN I THOUGHT...
YA SEE NOW, DOCTOR?
...I SIMPLY MOOST CLEAN MINE WINDOWS. THEY ARE TOTALLY FILTHY.

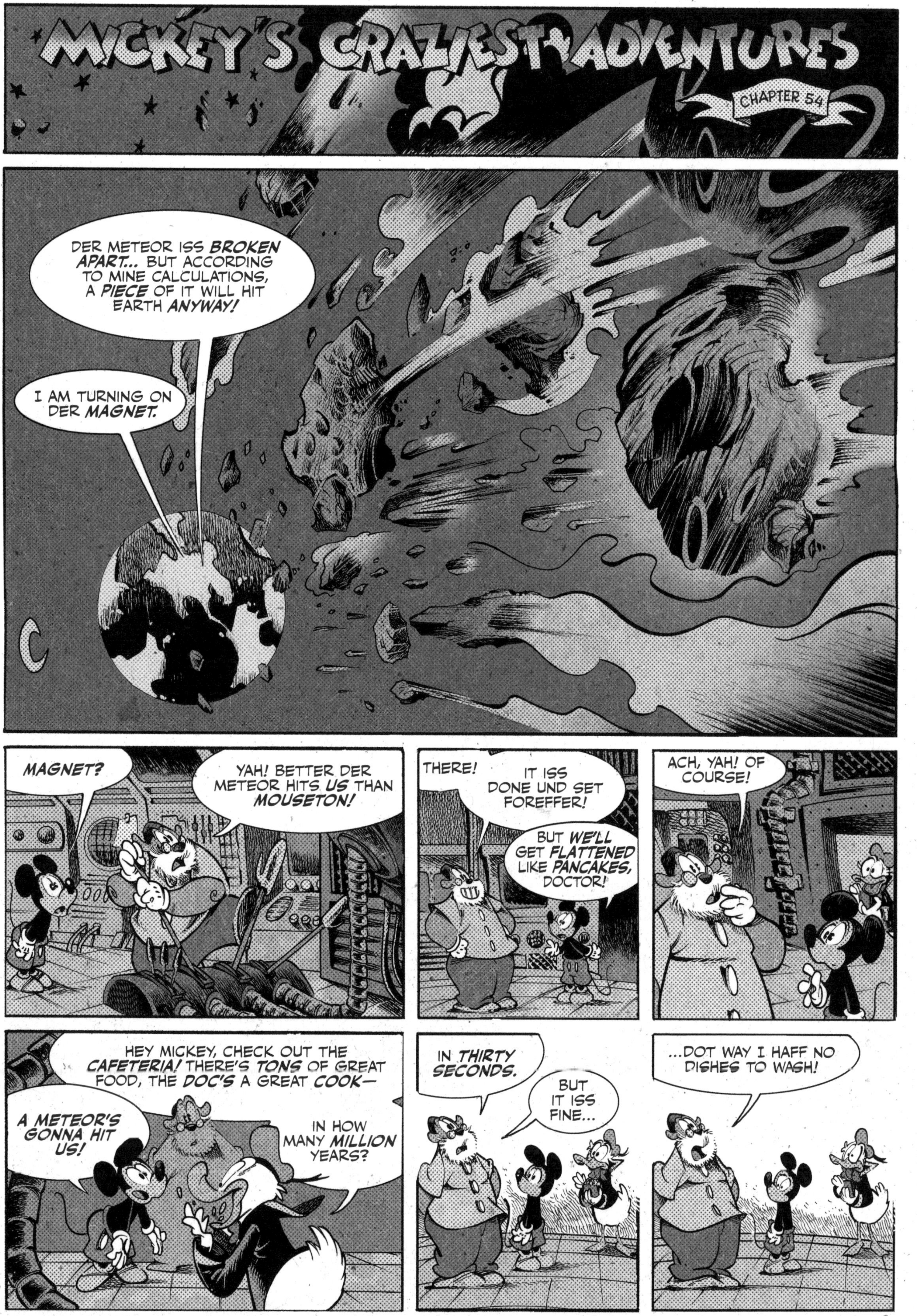
MICKEY'S CRAZIEST ADVENTURES
CHAPTER 54
DER METEOR ISS BROKEN APART... BUT ACCORDING TO MINE CALCULATIONS, A PIECE OF IT WILL HIT EARTH ANYWAY!
I AM TURNING ON DER MAGNET.
MAGNET?
YAH! BETTER DER METEOR HITS US THAN MOUSETON!
THERE!
IT ISS DONE UND SET FOREFFER!
BUT WE'LL GET FLATTENED LIKE PANCAKES, DOCTOR!
ACH, YAH! OF COURSE!
HEY MICKEY, CHECK OUT THE CAFETERIA! THERE'S TONS OF GREAT FOOD, THE DOC'S A GREAT COOK—
A METEOR'S GONNA HIT US!
IN HOW MANY MILLION YEARS?
IN THIRTY SECONDS.
BUT IT ISS FINE...
...DOT WAY I HAFF NO DISHES TO WASH!

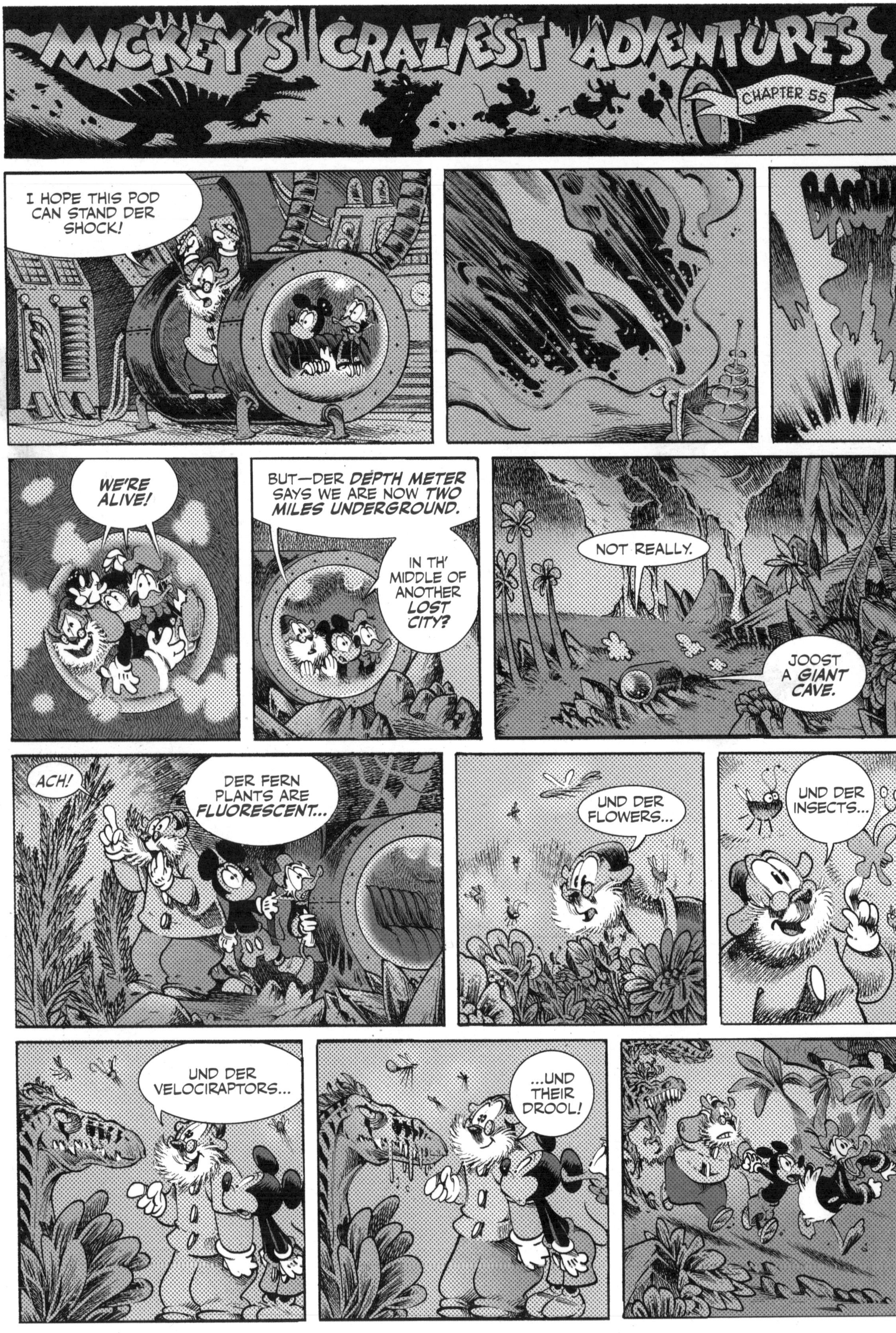
MICKEY'S CRAZIEST ADVENTURES
CHAPTER 55
I HOPE THIS POD CAN STAND DER SHOCK!
BAOOM
WE'RE ALIVE!
BUT—DER DEPTH METER SAYS WE ARE NOW TWO MILES UNDERGROUND.
IN TH' MIDDLE OF ANOTHER LOST CITY?
NOT REALLY.
JOOST A GIANT CAVE.
ACH!
DER FERN PLANTS ARE FLUORESCENT...
UND DER FLOWERS...
UND DER INSECTS...
UND DER VELOCIRAPTORS...
...UND THEIR DROOL!

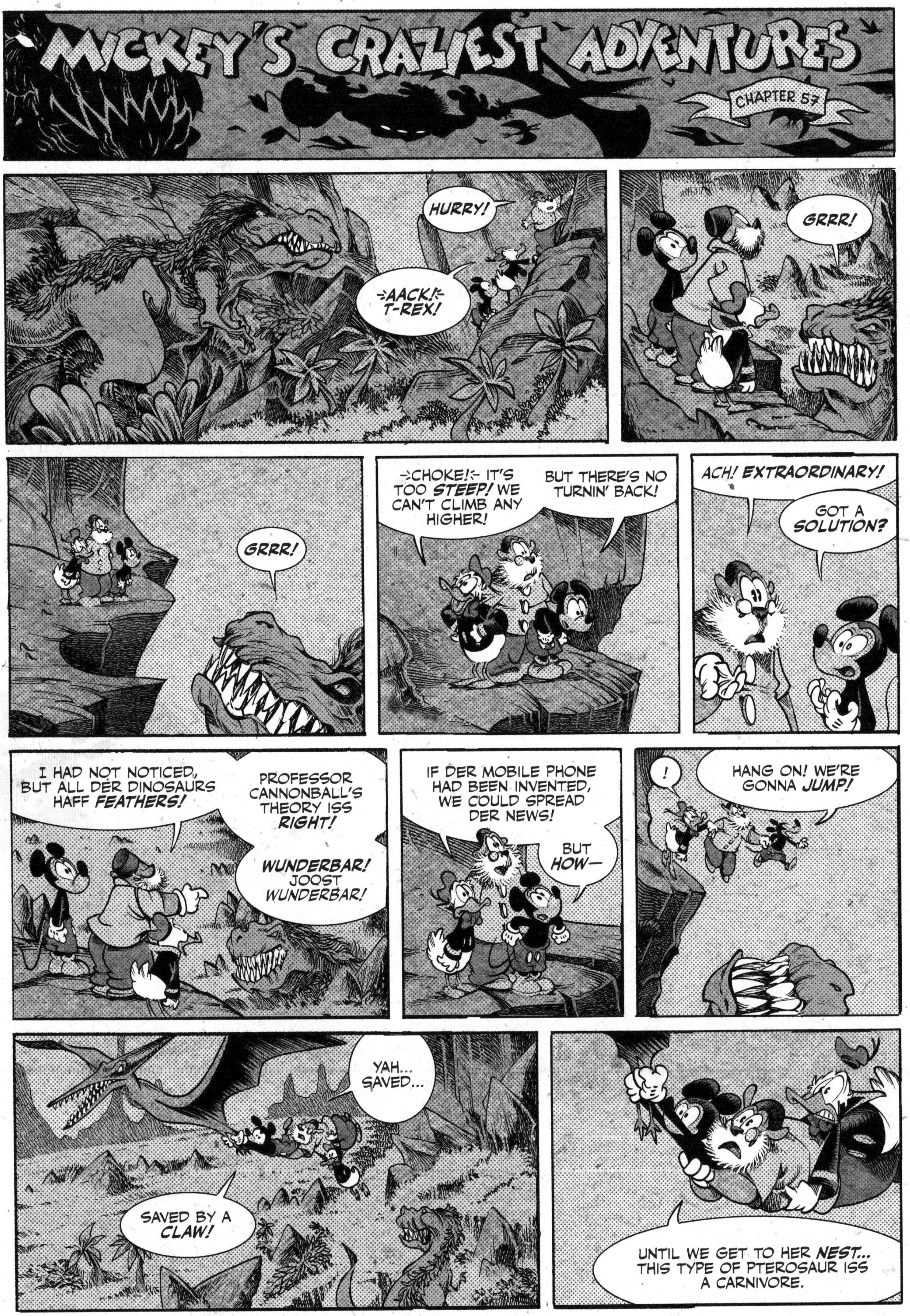
MICKEY'S CRAZIEST ADVENTURES
CHAPTER 57
HURRY!
-AACK!- T-REX!
GRRR!
GRRR!
-CHOKE!- IT'S TOO STEEP! WE CAN'T CLIMB ANY HIGHER!
BUT THERE'S NO TURNIN' BACK!
ACH! EXTRAORDINARY!
GOT A SOLUTION?
I HAD NOT NOTICED, BUT ALL DER DINOSAURS HAFF FEATHERS!
PROFESSOR CANNONBALL'S THEORY ISS RIGHT!
WUNDERBAR! JOOST WUNDERBAR!
IF DER MOBILE PHONE HAD BEEN INVENTED, WE COULD SPREAD DER NEWS!
BUT HOW—
!
HANG ON! WE'RE GONNA JUMP!
YAH... SAVED...
SAVED BY A CLAW!
UNTIL WE GET TO HER NEST... THIS TYPE OF PTEROSAUR ISS A CARNIVORE.

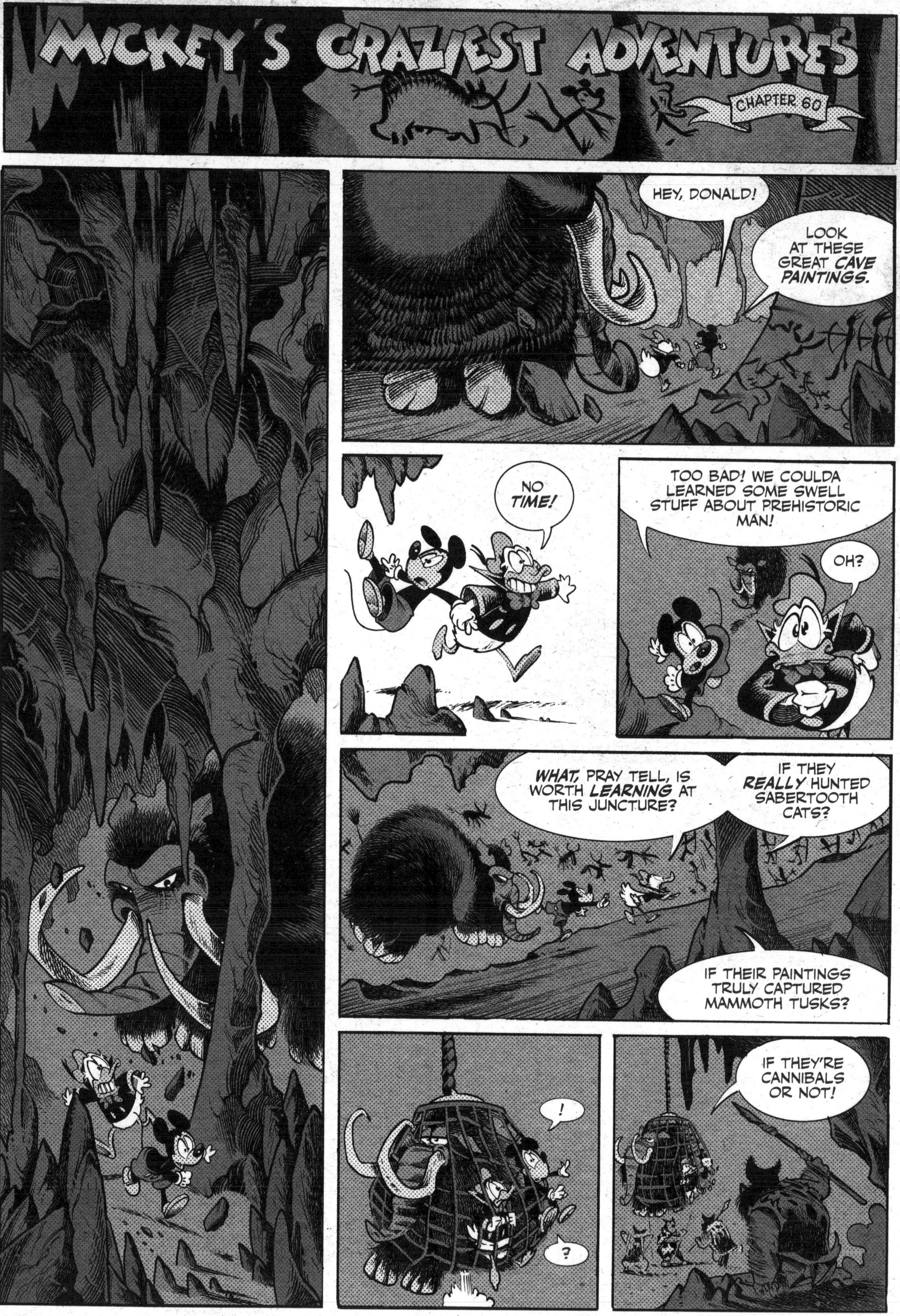
MICKEY'S CRAZIEST ADVENTURES
CHAPTER 60
HEY, DONALD!
LOOK AT THESE GREAT CAVE PAINTINGS.
NO TIME!
TOO BAD! WE COULDA LEARNED SOME SWELL STUFF ABOUT PREHISTORIC MAN!
OH?
WHAT, PRAY TELL, IS WORTH LEARNING AT THIS JUNCTURE?
IF THEY REALLY HUNTED SABERTOOTH CATS?
IF THEIR PAINTINGS TRULY CAPTURED MAMMOTH TUSKS?
!
?
IF THEY'RE CANNIBALS OR NOT!

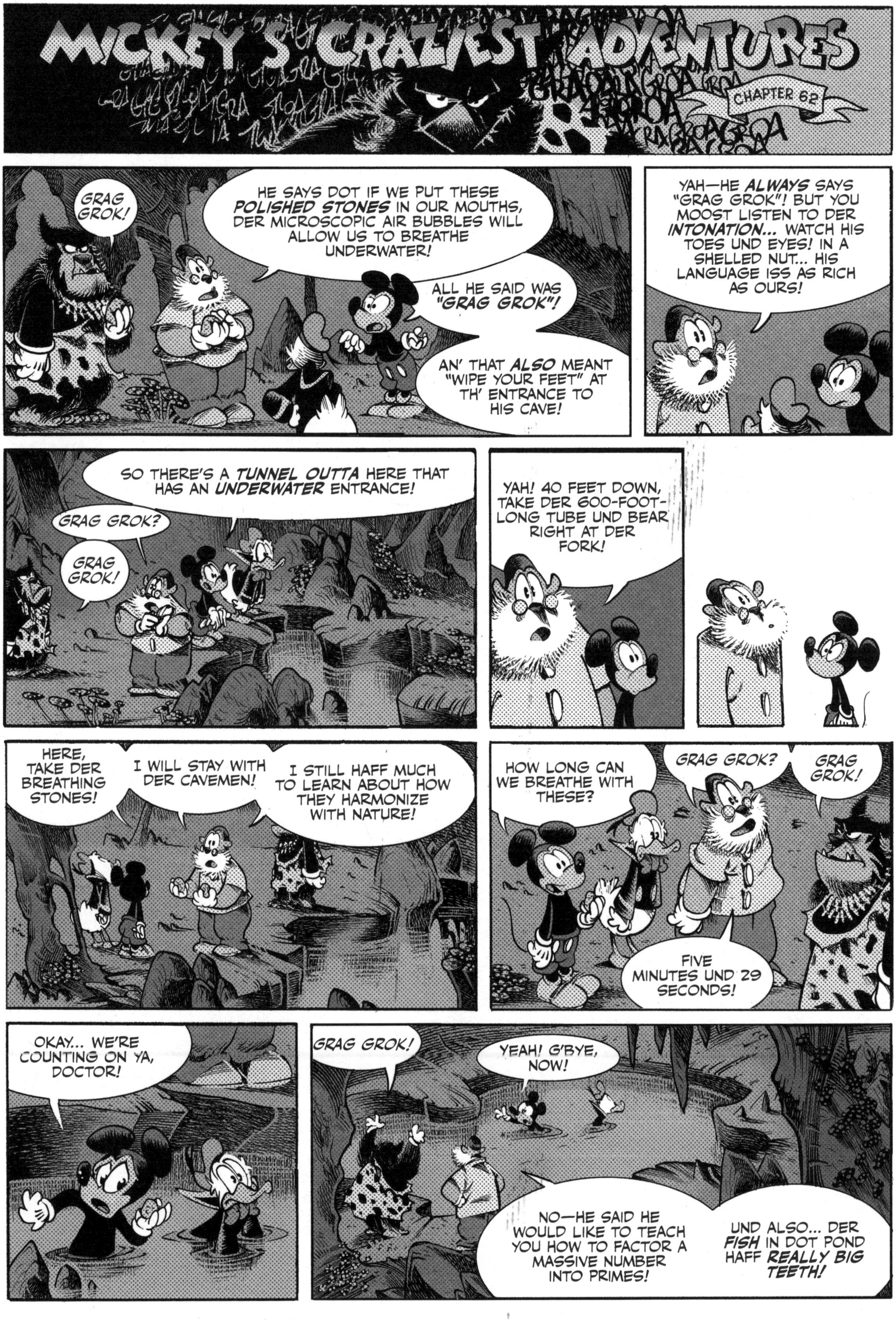
MICKEY'S CRAZIEST ADVENTURES
CHAPTER 62
GRAG GROK!
HE SAYS DOT IF WE PUT THESE POLISHED STONES IN OUR MOUTHS, DER MICROSCOPIC AIR BUBBLES WILL ALLOW US TO BREATHE UNDERWATER!
ALL HE SAID WAS "GRAG GROK"!
AN' THAT ALSO MEANT "WIPE YOUR FEET" AT TH' ENTRANCE TO HIS CAVE!
YAH—HE ALWAYS SAYS "GRAG GROK"! BUT YOU MOOST LISTEN TO DER INTONATION... WATCH HIS TOES UND EYES! IN A SHELLED NUT... HIS LANGUAGE ISS AS RICH AS OURS!
SO THERE'S A TUNNEL OUTTA HERE THAT HAS AN UNDERWATER ENTRANCE!
GRAG GROK?
GRAG GROK!
YAH! 40 FEET DOWN, TAKE DER 600-FOOT-LONG TUBE UND BEAR RIGHT AT DER FORK!
HERE, TAKE DER BREATHING STONES!
I WILL STAY WITH DER CAVEMEN!
I STILL HAFF MUCH TO LEARN ABOUT HOW THEY HARMONIZE WITH NATURE!
HOW LONG CAN WE BREATHE WITH THESE?
GRAG GROK?
GRAG GROK!
FIVE MINUTES UND 29 SECONDS!
OKAY... WE'RE COUNTING ON YA, DOCTOR!
GRAG GROK!
YEAH! G'BYE, NOW!
NO—HE SAID HE WOULD LIKE TO TEACH YOU HOW TO FACTOR A MASSIVE NUMBER INTO PRIMES!
UND ALSO... DER FISH IN DOT POND HAFF REALLY BIG TEETH!

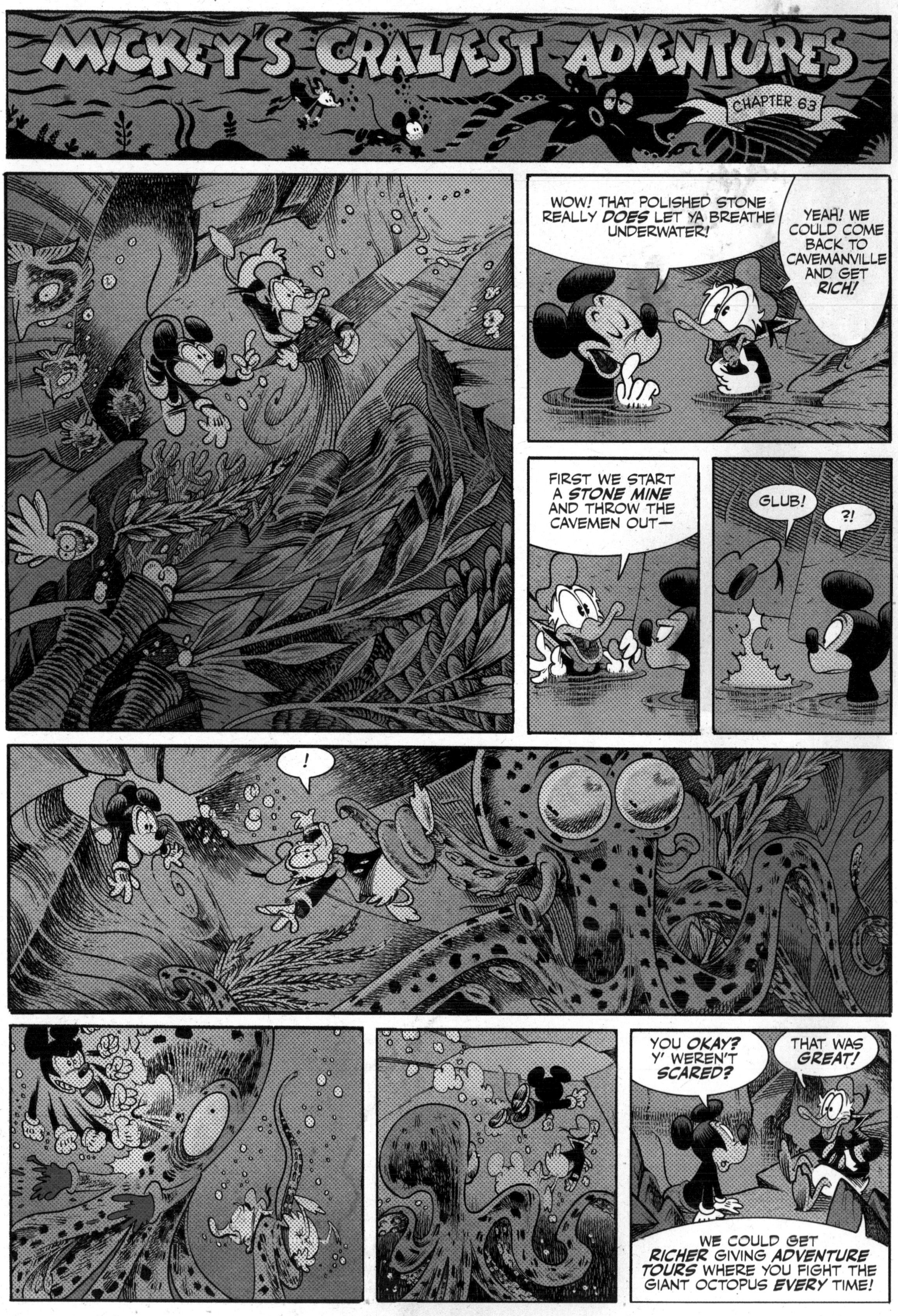
MICKEY'S CRAZIEST ADVENTURES
CHAPTER 63
WOW! THAT POLISHED STONE REALLY DOES LET YA BREATHE UNDERWATER!
YEAH! WE COULD COME BACK TO CAVEMANVILLE AND GET RICH!
FIRST WE START A STONE MINE AND THROW THE CAVEMEN OUT—
GLUB!
?!
!
YOU OKAY? Y' WEREN'T SCARED?
THAT WAS GREAT!
WE COULD GET RICHER GIVING ADVENTURE TOURS WHERE YOU FIGHT THE GIANT OCTOPUS EVERY TIME!

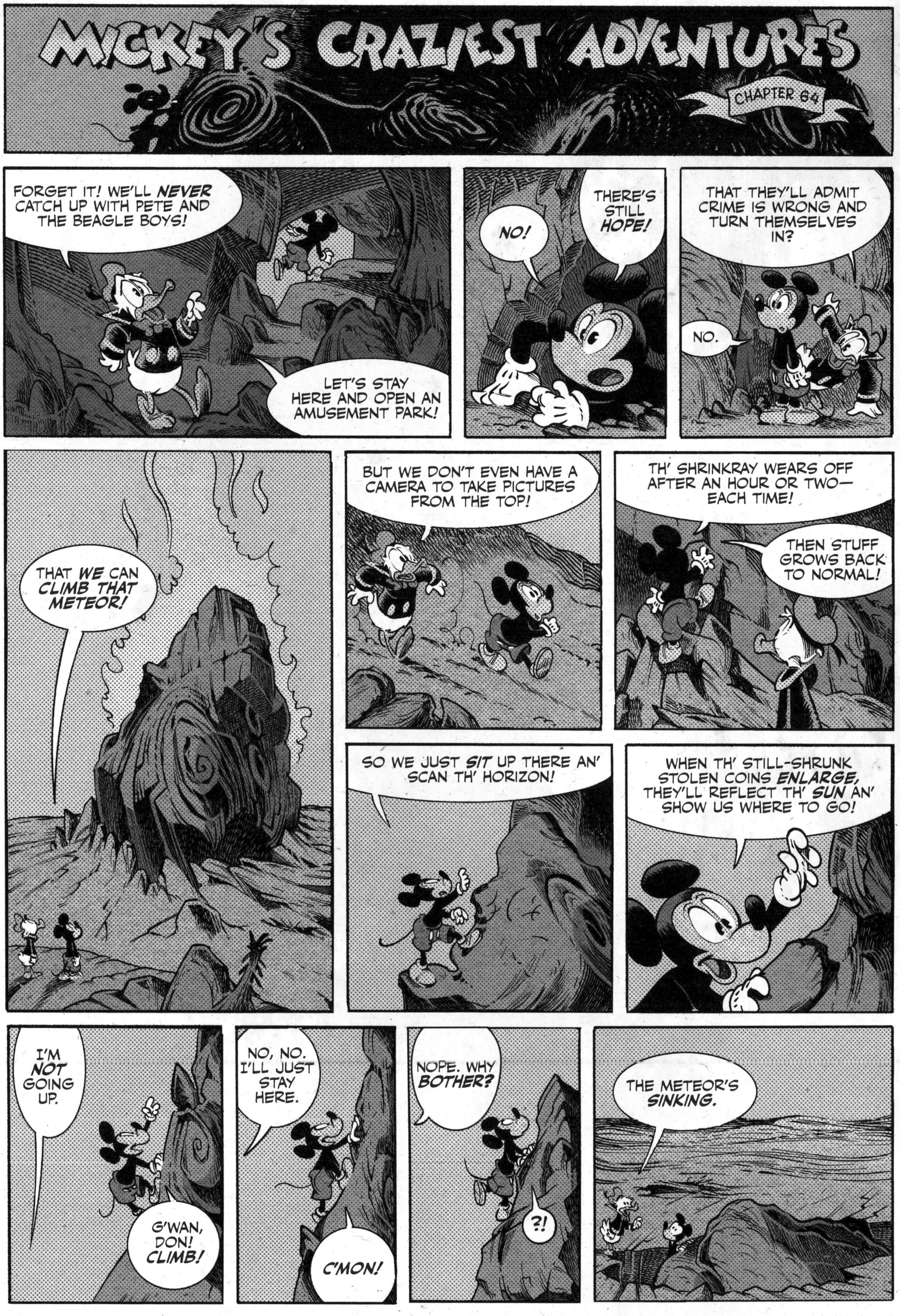
MICKEY'S CRAZIEST ADVENTURES
CHAPTER 64
FORGET IT! WE'LL NEVER CATCH UP WITH PETE AND THE BEAGLE BOYS!
LET'S STAY HERE AND OPEN AN AMUSEMENT PARK!
NO!
THERE'S STILL HOPE!
THAT THEY'LL ADMIT CRIME IS WRONG AND TURN THEMSELVES IN?
NO.
THAT WE CAN CLIMB THAT METEOR!
BUT WE DON'T EVEN HAVE A CAMERA TO TAKE PICTURES FROM THE TOP!
TH' SHRINKRAY WEARS OFF AFTER AN HOUR OR TWO— EACH TIME!
THEN STUFF GROWS BACK TO NORMAL!
SO WE JUST SIT UP THERE AN' SCAN TH' HORIZON!
WHEN TH' STILL-SHRUNK STOLEN COINS ENLARGE, THEY'LL REFLECT TH' SUN AN' SHOW US WHERE TO GO!
I'M NOT GOING UP.
G'WAN, DON! CLIMB!
NO, NO. I'LL JUST STAY HERE.
C'MON!
NOPE. WHY BOTHER?
?!
THE METEOR'S SINKING.

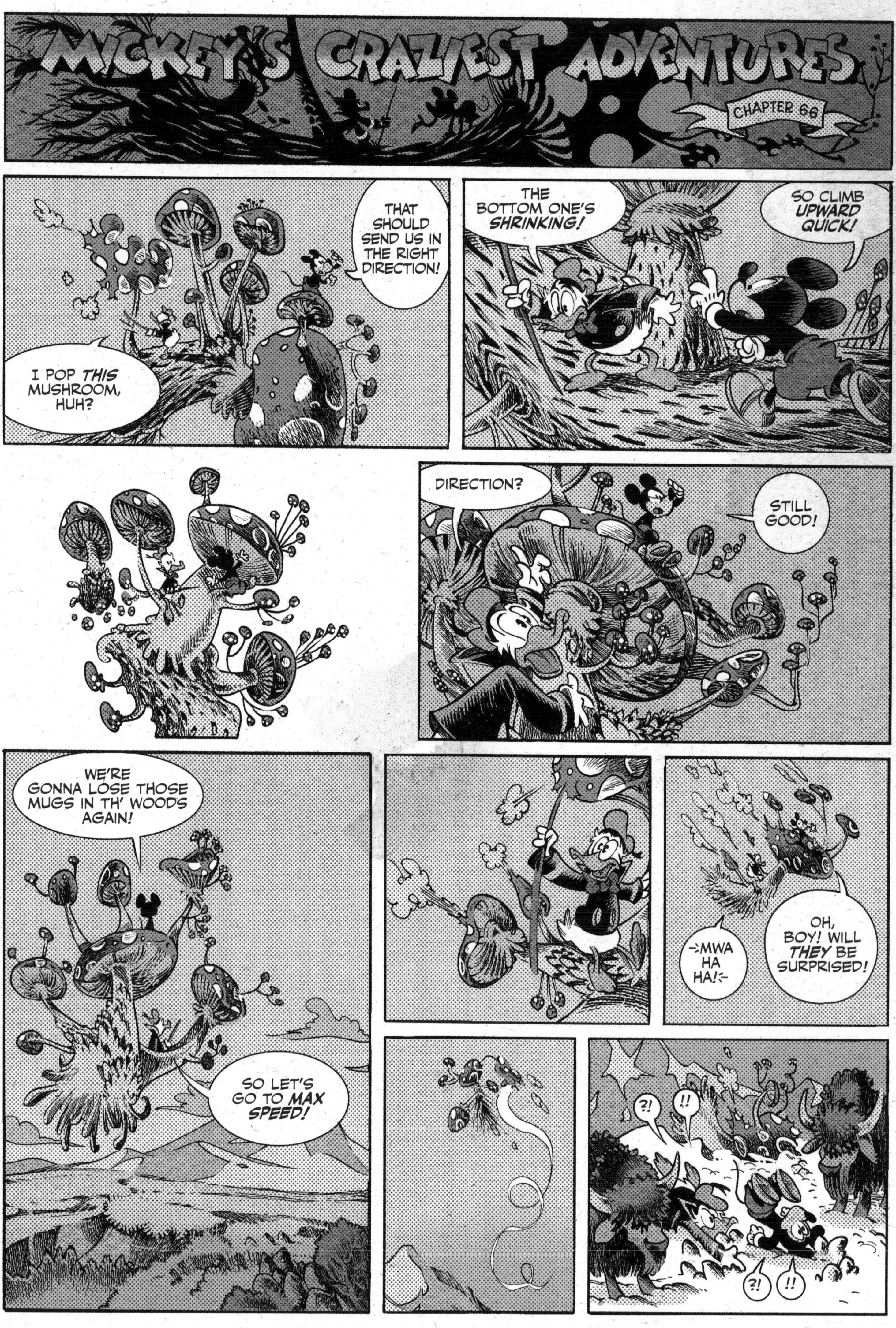
MICKEY'S CRAZIEST ADVENTURES
CHAPTER 66
THAT SHOULD SEND US IN THE RIGHT DIRECTION!
I POP THIS MUSHROOM, HUH?
THE BOTTOM ONE'S SHRINKING!
SO CLIMB UPWARD QUICK!
DIRECTION?
STILL GOOD!
WE'RE GONNA LOSE THOSE MUGS IN TH' WOODS AGAIN!
SO LET'S GO TO MAX SPEED!
OH, BOY! WILL THEY BE SURPRISED!
MWA HA HA!
?!
!!
?!
!!

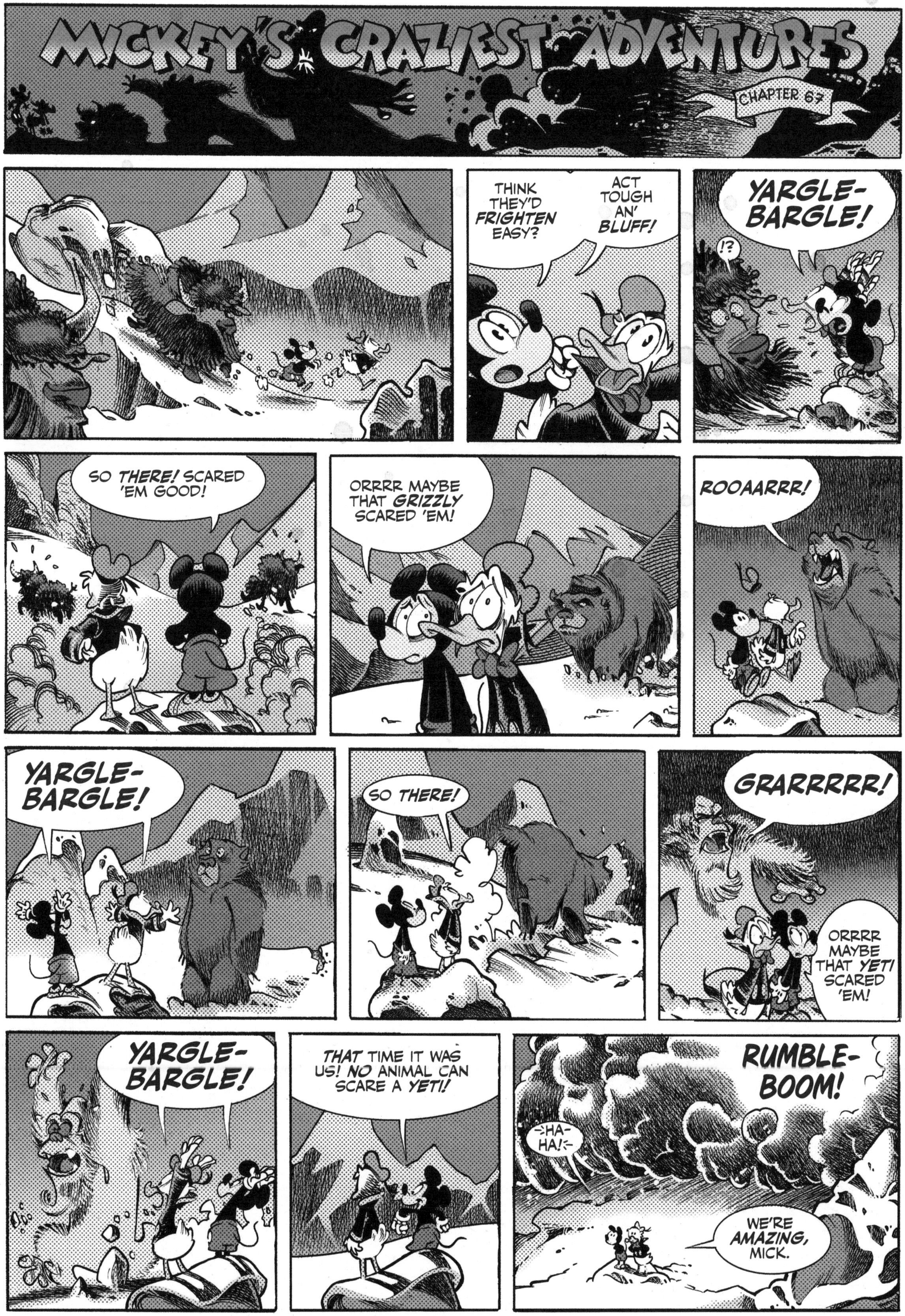
MICKEY'S CRAZIEST ADVENTURES
CHAPTER 67
THINK THEY'D FRIGHTEN EASY?
ACT TOUGH AN' BLUFF!
YARGLE-BARGLE!
!?
SO THERE! SCARED 'EM GOOD!
ORRRR MAYBE THAT GRIZZLY SCARED 'EM!
ROOAARRR!
YARGLE-BARGLE!
SO THERE!
GRARRRRR!
ORRRR MAYBE THAT YETI SCARED 'EM!
YARGLE-BARGLE!
THAT TIME IT WAS US! NO ANIMAL CAN SCARE A YETI!
RUMBLE-BOOM!
HA-HA!
WE'RE AMAZING, MICK.

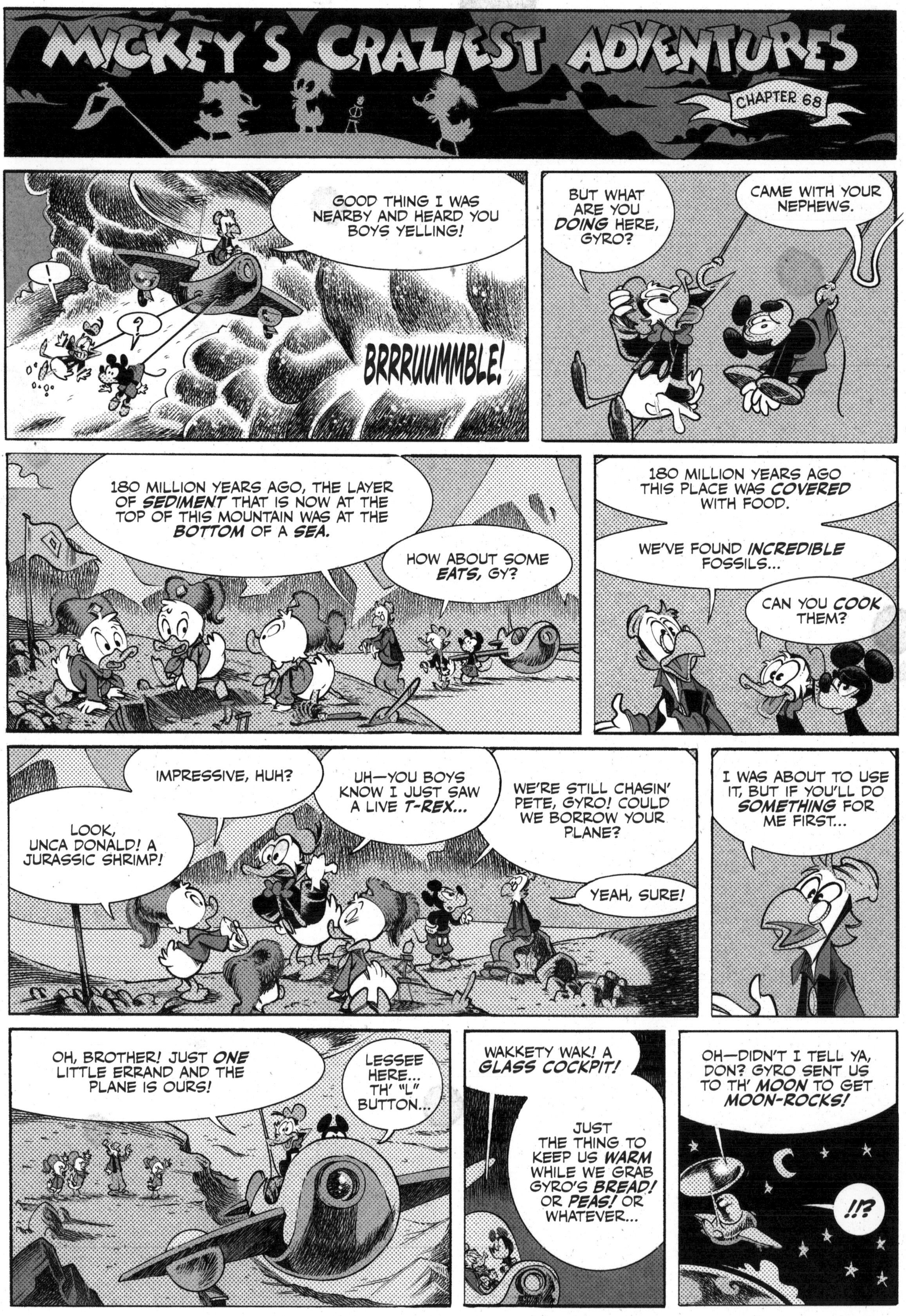
MICKEY'S CRAZIEST ADVENTURES
CHAPTER 68
GOOD THING I WAS NEARBY AND HEARD YOU BOYS YELLING!
!
?
BRRRUUMMBLE!
BUT WHAT ARE YOU DOING HERE, GYRO?
CAME WITH YOUR NEPHEWS.
180 MILLION YEARS AGO, THE LAYER OF SEDIMENT THAT IS NOW AT THE TOP OF THIS MOUNTAIN WAS AT THE BOTTOM OF A SEA.
HOW ABOUT SOME EATS, GY?
180 MILLION YEARS AGO THIS PLACE WAS COVERED WITH FOOD.
WE'VE FOUND INCREDIBLE FOSSILS...
CAN YOU COOK THEM?
IMPRESSIVE, HUH?
LOOK, UNCA DONALD! A JURASSIC SHRIMP!
UH—YOU BOYS KNOW I JUST SAW A LIVE T-REX...
WE'RE STILL CHASIN' PETE, GYRO! COULD WE BORROW YOUR PLANE?
YEAH, SURE!
I WAS ABOUT TO USE IT, BUT IF YOU'LL DO SOMETHING FOR ME FIRST...
OH, BROTHER! JUST ONE LITTLE ERRAND AND THE PLANE IS OURS!
LESSEE HERE... TH' "L" BUTTON...
WAKKETY WAK! A GLASS COCKPIT!
JUST THE THING TO KEEP US WARM WHILE WE GRAB GYRO'S BREAD! OR PEAS! OR WHATEVER...
OH—DIDN'T I TELL YA, DON? GYRO SENT US TO TH' MOON TO GET MOON-ROCKS!
!!?

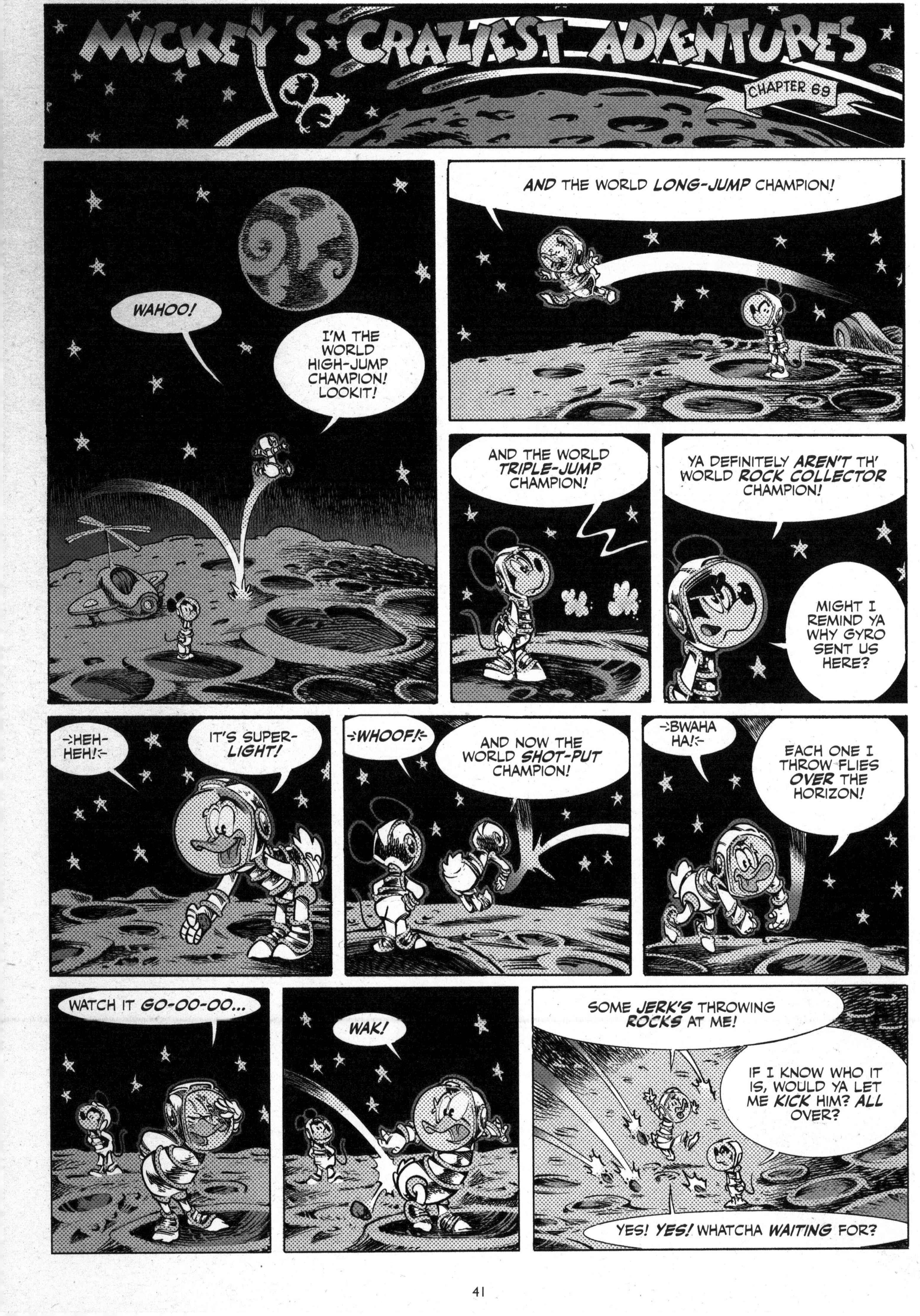
MICKEY'S CRAZIEST ADVENTURES
CHAPTER 69
WAHOO!
I'M THE WORLD HIGH-JUMP CHAMPION! LOOKIT!
AND THE WORLD LONG-JUMP CHAMPION!
AND THE WORLD TRIPLE-JUMP CHAMPION!
YA DEFINITELY AREN'T TH' WORLD ROCK COLLECTOR CHAMPION!
MIGHT I REMIND YA WHY GYRO SENT US HERE?
-HEH-HEH!-
IT'S SUPER-LIGHT!
-WHOOF!-
AND NOW THE WORLD SHOT-PUT CHAMPION!
-BWAHA HA!-
EACH ONE I THROW FLIES OVER THE HORIZON!
WATCH IT GO-OO-OO...
WAK!
SOME JERK'S THROWING ROCKS AT ME!
IF I KNOW WHO IT IS, WOULD YA LET ME KICK HIM? ALL OVER?
YES! YES! WHATCHA WAITING FOR?

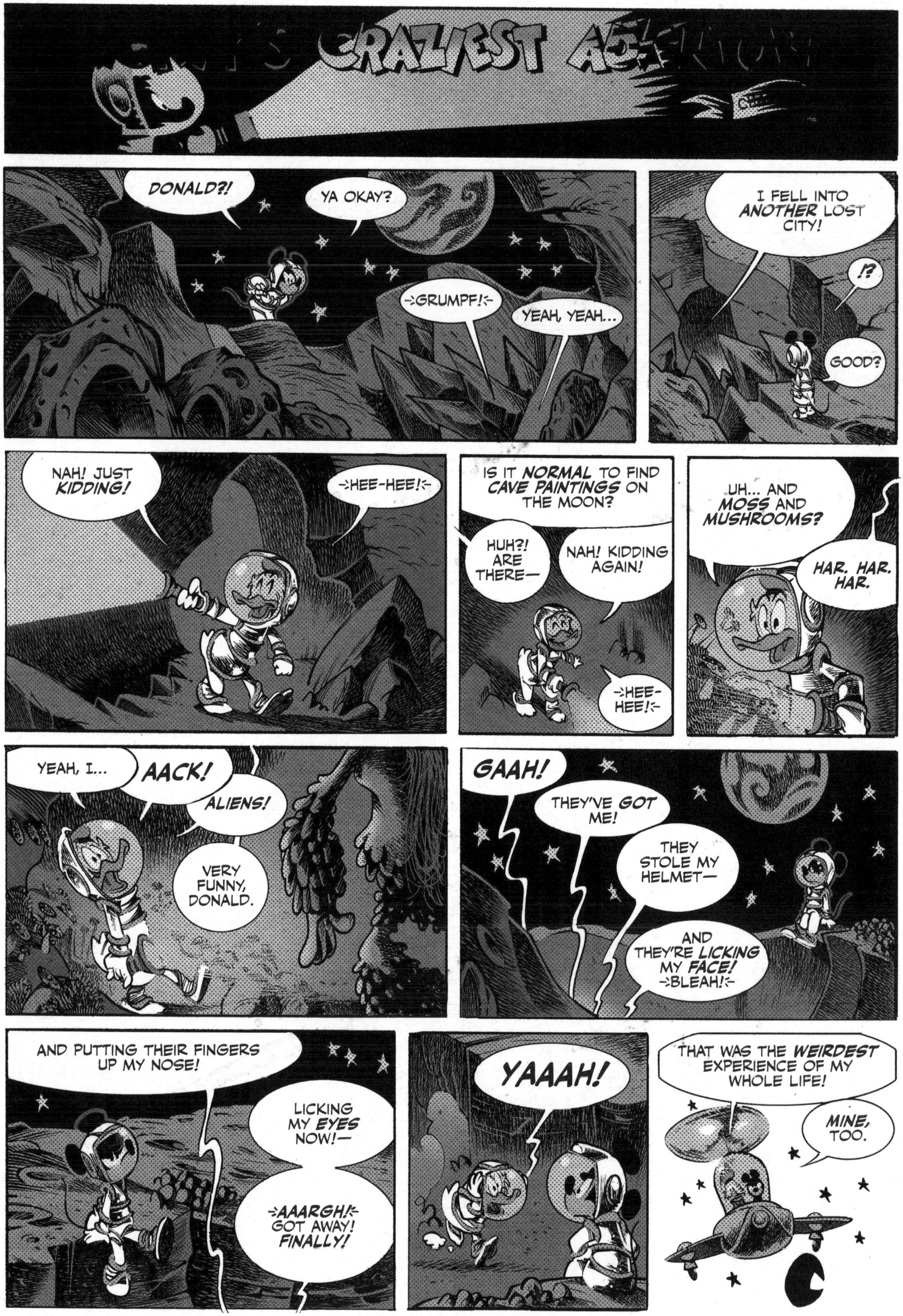
CRAZIEST
DONALD?!
YA OKAY?
-GRUMPF!-
YEAH, YEAH...
I FELL INTO ANOTHER LOST CITY!
!?
GOOD?
NAH! JUST KIDDING!
-HEE-HEE!-
IS IT NORMAL TO FIND CAVE PAINTINGS ON THE MOON?
HUH?! ARE THERE—
NAH! KIDDING AGAIN!
-HEE-HEE!-
UH... AND MOSS AND MUSHROOMS?
HAR. HAR. HAR.
YEAH, I...
AACK!
ALIENS!
VERY FUNNY, DONALD.
GAAH!
THEY'VE GOT ME!
THEY STOLE MY HELMET—
AND THEY'RE LICKING MY FACE! -BLEAH!-
AND PUTTING THEIR FINGERS UP MY NOSE!
LICKING MY EYES NOW!—
-AAARGH!- GOT AWAY! FINALLY!
YAAAH!
THAT WAS THE WEIRDEST EXPERIENCE OF MY WHOLE LIFE!
MINE, TOO.

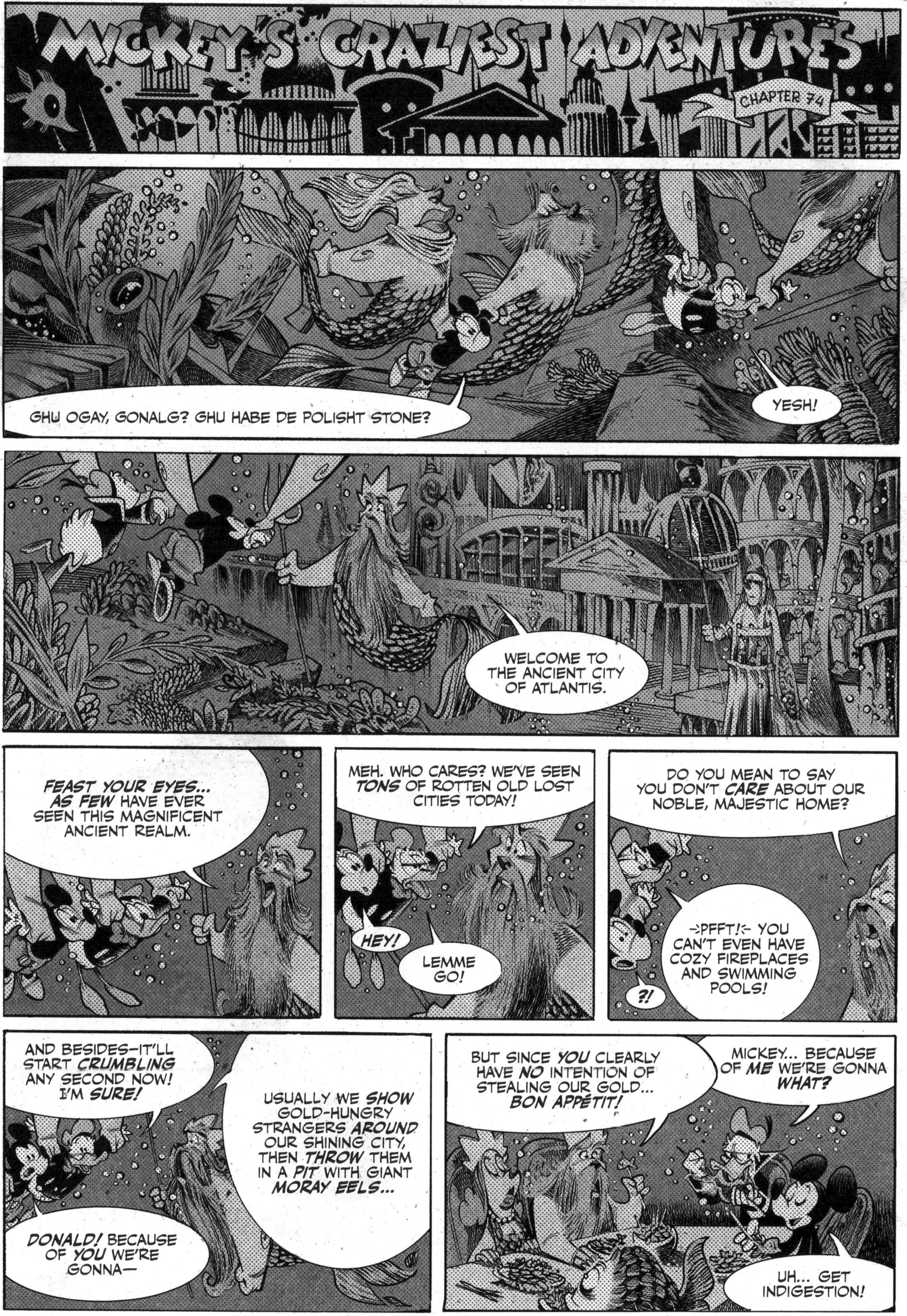
MICKEY'S CRAZIEST ADVENTURES
CHAPTER 74
GHU OGAY, GONALG? GHU HABE DE POLISHT STONE?
YESH!
WELCOME TO THE ANCIENT CITY OF ATLANTIS.
FEAST YOUR EYES... AS FEW HAVE EVER SEEN THIS MAGNIFICENT ANCIENT REALM.
MEH. WHO CARES? WE'VE SEEN TONS OF ROTTEN OLD LOST CITIES TODAY!
HEY!
LEMME GO!
DO YOU MEAN TO SAY YOU DON'T CARE ABOUT OUR NOBLE, MAJESTIC HOME?
-PFFT!- YOU CAN'T EVEN HAVE COZY FIREPLACES AND SWIMMING POOLS!
?!
AND BESIDES—IT'LL START CRUMBLING ANY SECOND NOW! I'M SURE!
USUALLY WE SHOW GOLD-HUNGRY STRANGERS AROUND OUR SHINING CITY, THEN THROW THEM IN A PIT WITH GIANT MORAY EELS...
DONALD! BECAUSE OF YOU WE'RE GONNA—
BUT SINCE YOU CLEARLY HAVE NO INTENTION OF STEALING OUR GOLD... BON APPÉTIT!
MICKEY... BECAUSE OF ME WE'RE GONNA WHAT?
UH... GET INDIGESTION!

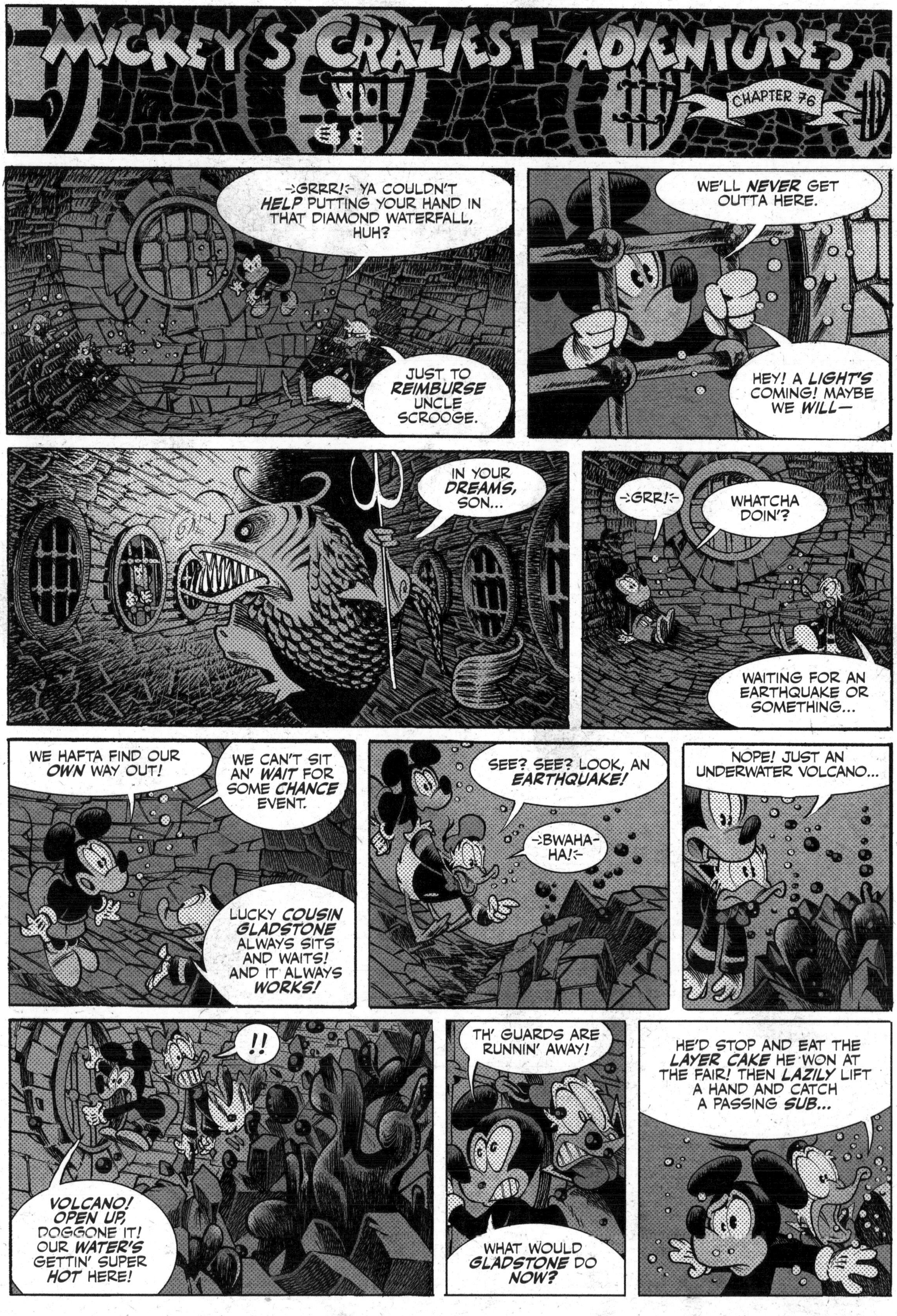
MICKEY'S CRAZIEST ADVENTURES
CHAPTER 76
-GRRR!- YA COULDN'T HELP PUTTING YOUR HAND IN THAT DIAMOND WATERFALL, HUH?
JUST TO REIMBURSE UNCLE SCROOGE.
WE'LL NEVER GET OUTTA HERE.
HEY! A LIGHT'S COMING! MAYBE WE WILL—
IN YOUR DREAMS, SON...
-GRR!-
WHATCHA DOIN'?
WAITING FOR AN EARTHQUAKE OR SOMETHING...
WE HAFTA FIND OUR OWN WAY OUT!
WE CAN'T SIT AN' WAIT FOR SOME CHANCE EVENT.
LUCKY COUSIN GLADSTONE ALWAYS SITS AND WAITS! AND IT ALWAYS WORKS!
SEE? SEE? LOOK, AN EARTHQUAKE!
-BWAHA-HA!-
NOPE! JUST AN UNDERWATER VOLCANO...
!!
VOLCANO! OPEN UP, DOGGONE IT! OUR WATER'S GETTIN' SUPER HOT HERE!
TH' GUARDS ARE RUNNIN' AWAY!
WHAT WOULD GLADSTONE DO NOW?
HE'D STOP AND EAT THE LAYER CAKE HE WON AT THE FAIR! THEN LAZILY LIFT A HAND AND CATCH A PASSING SUB...

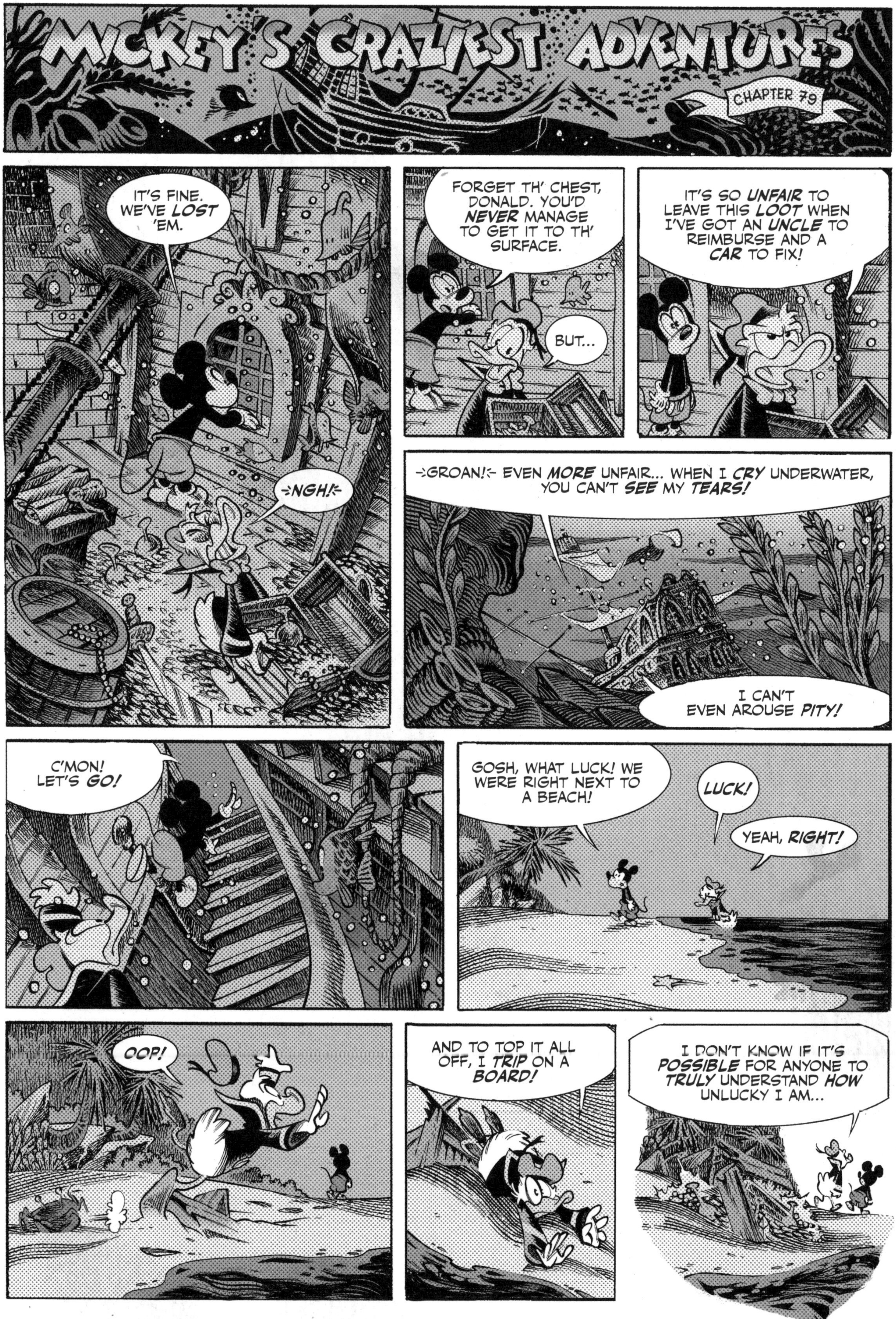
MICKEY'S CRAZIEST ADVENTURES
CHAPTER 79
IT'S FINE. WE'VE LOST 'EM.
-NGH!-
FORGET TH' CHEST, DONALD. YOU'D NEVER MANAGE TO GET IT TO TH' SURFACE.
BUT...
IT'S SO UNFAIR TO LEAVE THIS LOOT WHEN I'VE GOT AN UNCLE TO REIMBURSE AND A CAR TO FIX!
-GROAN!- EVEN MORE UNFAIR... WHEN I CRY UNDERWATER, YOU CAN'T SEE MY TEARS!
I CAN'T EVEN AROUSE PITY!
C'MON! LET'S GO!
GOSH, WHAT LUCK! WE WERE RIGHT NEXT TO A BEACH!
LUCK!
YEAH, RIGHT!
OOP!
AND TO TOP IT ALL OFF, I TRIP ON A BOARD!
I DON'T KNOW IF IT'S POSSIBLE FOR ANYONE TO TRULY UNDERSTAND HOW UNLUCKY I AM...

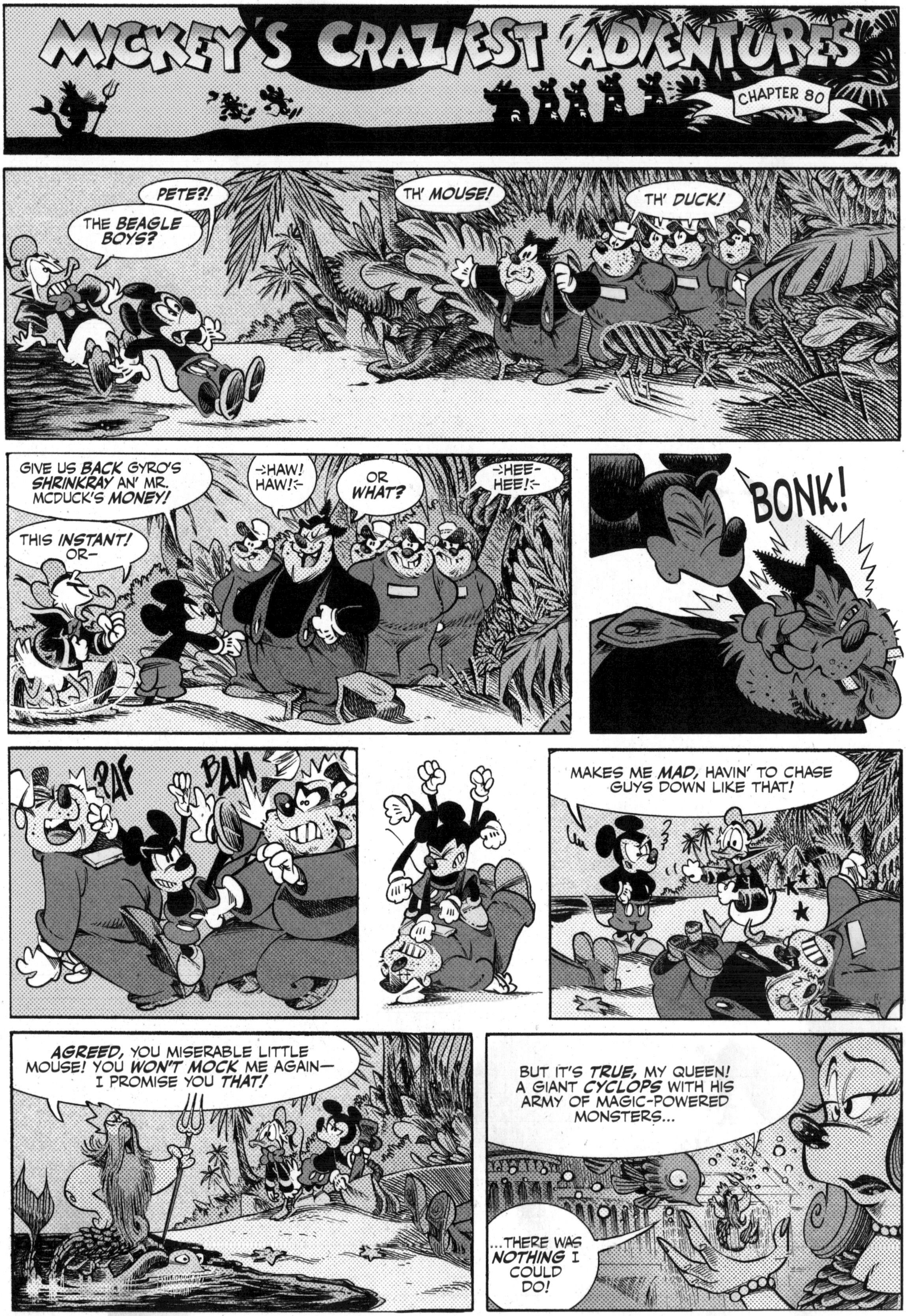
MICKEY'S CRAZIEST ADVENTURES
CHAPTER 80
PETE?!
THE BEAGLE BOYS?
TH' MOUSE!
TH' DUCK!
GIVE US BACK GYRO'S SHRINKRAY AN' MR. MCDUCK'S MONEY!
THIS INSTANT! OR–
HAW! HAW!
OR WHAT?
HEE-HEE!
BONK!
PAF
BAM
MAKES ME MAD, HAVIN' TO CHASE GUYS DOWN LIKE THAT!
AGREED, YOU MISERABLE LITTLE MOUSE! YOU WON'T MOCK ME AGAIN— I PROMISE YOU THAT!
BUT IT'S TRUE, MY QUEEN! A GIANT CYCLOPS WITH HIS ARMY OF MAGIC-POWERED MONSTERS...
...THERE WAS NOTHING I COULD DO!

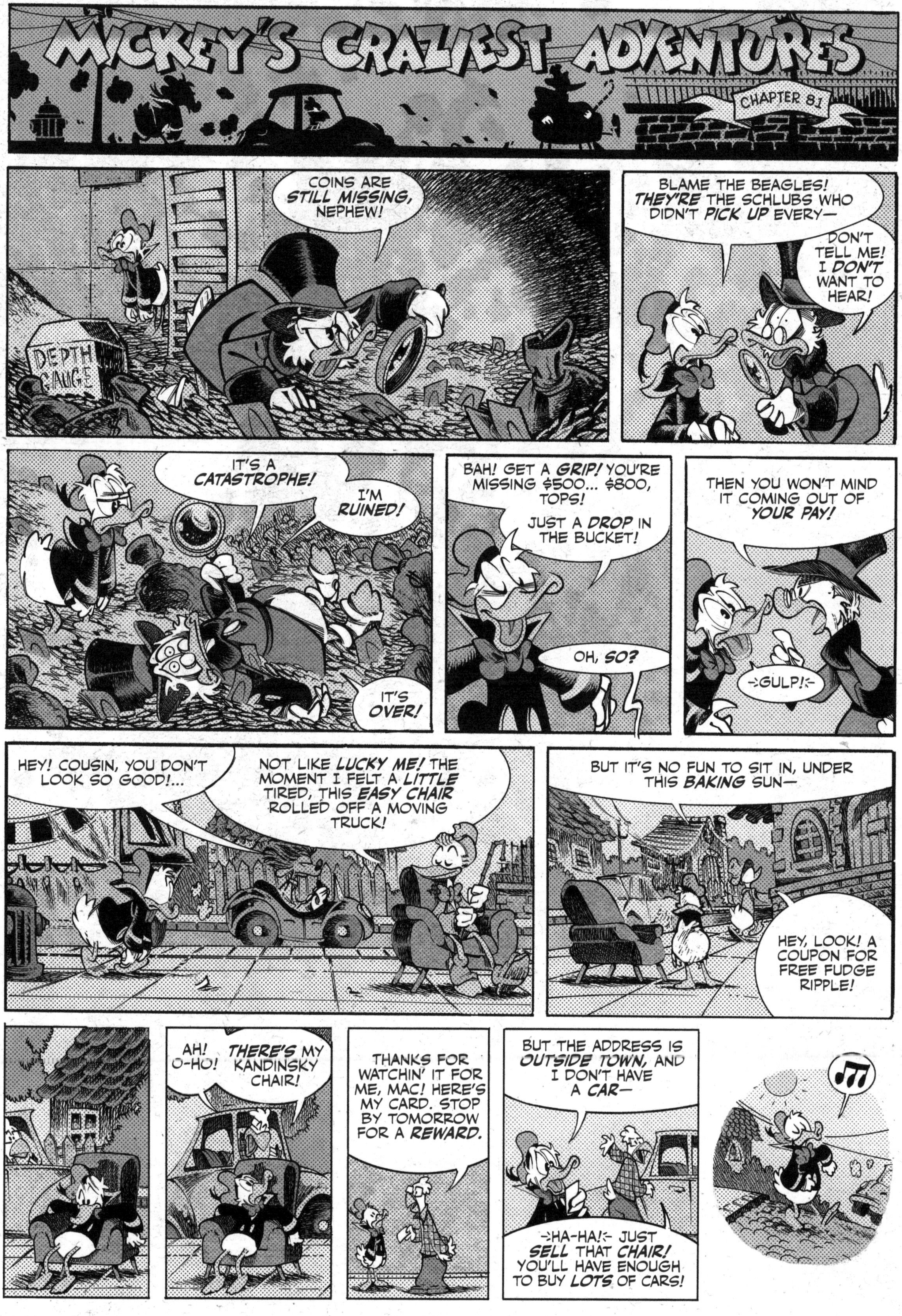
MICKEY'S CRAZIEST ADVENTURES
CHAPTER 81
DEPTH GAUGE
COINS ARE STILL MISSING, NEPHEW!
BLAME THE BEAGLES! THEY'RE THE SCHLUBS WHO DIDN'T PICK UP EVERY—
DON'T TELL ME! I DON'T WANT TO HEAR!
IT'S A CATASTROPHE!
I'M RUINED!
IT'S OVER!
BAH! GET A GRIP! YOU'RE MISSING $500... $800, TOPS!
JUST A DROP IN THE BUCKET!
OH, SO?
THEN YOU WON'T MIND IT COMING OUT OF YOUR PAY!
GULP!
HEY! COUSIN, YOU DON'T LOOK SO GOOD!...
NOT LIKE LUCKY ME! THE MOMENT I FELT A LITTLE TIRED, THIS EASY CHAIR ROLLED OFF A MOVING TRUCK!
BUT IT'S NO FUN TO SIT IN, UNDER THIS BAKING SUN—
HEY, LOOK! A COUPON FOR FREE FUDGE RIPPLE!
AH! O-HO!
THERE'S MY KANDINSKY CHAIR!
THANKS FOR WATCHIN' IT FOR ME, MAC! HERE'S MY CARD. STOP BY TOMORROW FOR A REWARD.
BUT THE ADDRESS IS OUTSIDE TOWN, AND I DON'T HAVE A CAR—
HA-HA! JUST SELL THAT CHAIR! YOU'LL HAVE ENOUGH TO BUY LOTS OF CARS!

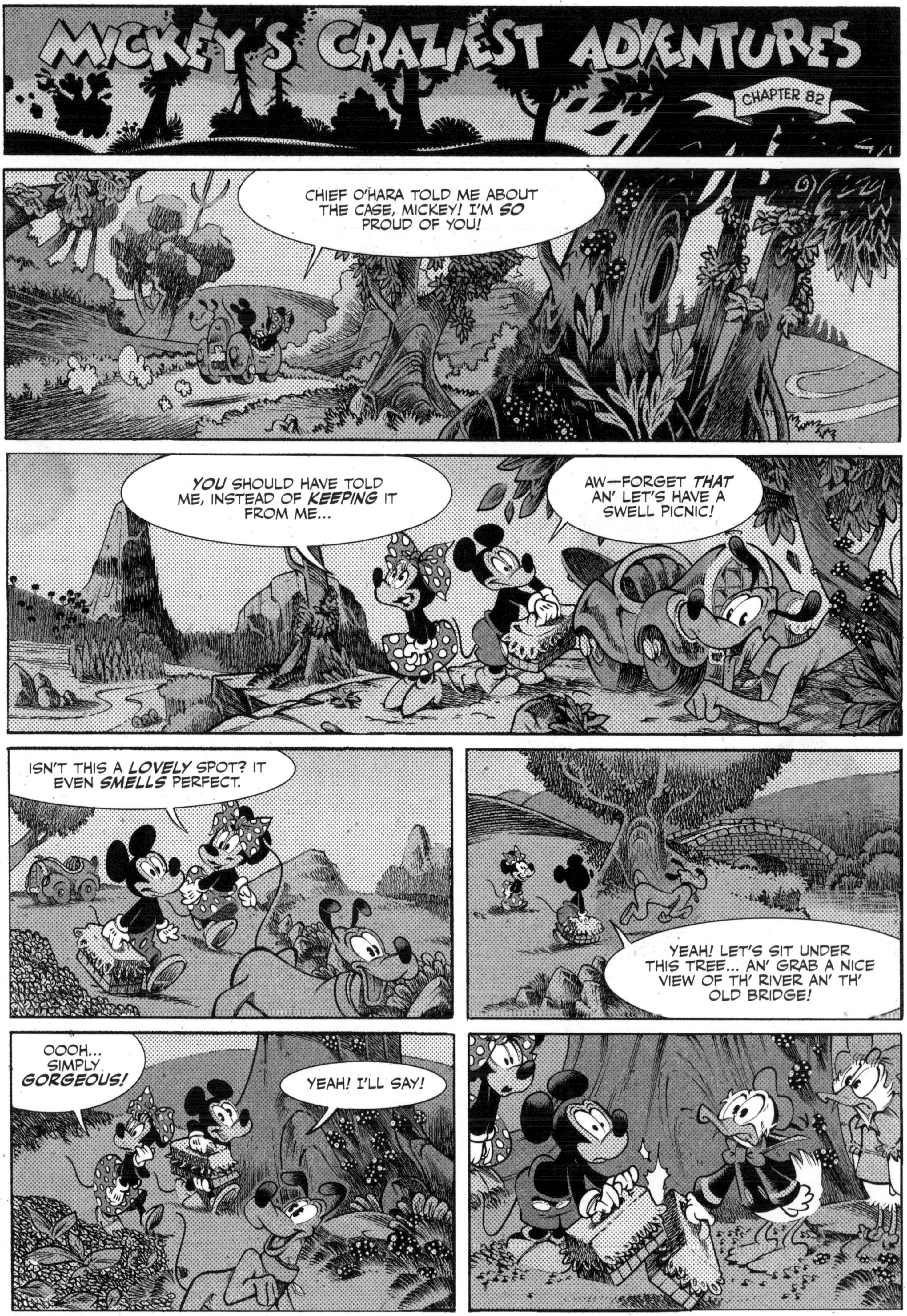
MICKEY'S CRAZIEST ADVENTURES
CHAPTER 82
CHIEF O'HARA TOLD ME ABOUT THE CASE, MICKEY! I'M SO PROUD OF YOU!
YOU SHOULD HAVE TOLD ME, INSTEAD OF KEEPING IT FROM ME...
AW—FORGET THAT AN' LET'S HAVE A SWELL PICNIC!
ISN'T THIS A LOVELY SPOT? IT EVEN SMELLS PERFECT.
YEAH! LET'S SIT UNDER THIS TREE... AN' GRAB A NICE VIEW OF TH' RIVER AN' TH' OLD BRIDGE!
OOOH... SIMPLY GORGEOUS!
YEAH! I'LL SAY!